Negro Militia
and Reconstruction

D1536975

Negro Militia
and Reconstruction

By Otis A. Singletary

Austin • University of Texas Press

Library of Congress Control Number 57-007559

ISBN 978-0-292-74176-8, paperback

For Francis Butler Simkins

Foreword

THE PASSAGE of the first Reconstruction Act on March 2, 1867, marked the climax of a long and bitter struggle between the executive and legislative branches of the federal government over the right to determine and to implement the policies by means of which the Southern states were to be reconstructed. Prior to that date, the program had been almost exclusive property of the executive department. Presidents Lincoln and Johnson followed a course which was essentially dedicated to the immediate and relatively painless restoration of these states to their erstwhile position in the Union.

In the two years following the Civil War during which the presidents dominated the Reconstruction process, congressional opposition steadily grew; this opposition eventually solidified and in March, 1867, through a series of laws known collectively as the Reconstruction acts, over-all direction was abruptly taken out of the hands of the President and assumed by Congress. The ensuing program contained the seeds of social revolution for the South. It is not surprising, therefore, that the years after 1867 were marked by serious dislocations and aberrations, the ugliest of which was an angry wave of racial violence.

A not inconsiderable amount of this violence was directly connected with the Negro militia movement. In most Southern states these troops originated as a defensive force; they were the protective arm of the newly created Radical state administrations. Since a powerful element among Southern whites remained implacable in their opposition to these governments, the need for protection was a very real one indeed.

In so far as its purpose was the perpetuation of Radical

state governments, the militia experiment can be fairly adjudged a failure. Such failures, however, are frequently as instructive to the historian as those more fortunate movements which are rewarded with success, for they, too, are inextricably woven into the historical fabric of the period. Yet, even if this were not true, the story of the Negro militia movement, intricate in design and colorful in execution, would still be worth telling, particularly in our own day, when thoughtful persons have reason to fear a resurgence of racial violence in the South.

To many persons who have, in one way or another, aided me in this work, I here express my appreciation. Without involving them in any way in responsibility for my views or for any errors, I particularly wish to thank Professors Francis B. Simkins, of Longwood College; Bell I. Wiley, of Emory University; and T. Harry Williams, of Louisiana State University. To my wife, Gloria, I am indebted for the performance of such unrewarding chores as typing and proofreading. Publication of this manuscript was encouraged by the American Military Institute and was facilitated by a grant from the Research Institute of the University of Texas.

OTIS A. SINGLETARY

Austin, Texas
January 15, 1957

Contents

Illustrations

Negro Militia
and Reconstruction

I. Genesis of the Militia Movement

WHEN THE DEFINITIVE ACCOUNT of the South during Reconstruction is finally written, it will contain deep and depressing undertones of violence. The long-standing and lamentable Southern tendency in this direction, which has already brought down adverse judgments of several generations of historians, only partially explains its prevalence during the period following the Civil War. Add to this historical predisposition the social unrest that inevitably follows military conquest, the perplexing new social, economic, and political problems associated with the freedmen, and the presence of a large number of men well schooled in the art of killing and grown sullen from tasting the bitterness of defeat, and a formula emerges that at least begins to explain why Reconstruction was pre-eminently a period of violence.

When Charles Nordhoff made his observation tour of the South in 1875, he expressed amazement in finding that not only the men but even boys of fourteen were frequently armed and that "every trifling dispute" was "ended with the pistol."[1] One of the innumerable Senate investigating committees which held hearings in the South was shocked to discover that carrying arms was an almost universal practice there. Many witnesses appeared before the group fully armed; and when the committee returned to the relatively peaceful environs of the nation's Capitol, they described the region as "the greatest place on the face of the earth for pistols" and asserted that "no man is comfortable down there unless he has got his pistols."[2] The novelist

[1] Charles Nordhoff, *The Cotton States in the Spring and Summer of 1875*, p. 78.
[2] S. Rep. 527, 44th Cong., 1st Sess., p. 56.

Negro Militia and Reconstruction

Albion W. Tourgee, a disillusioned participant in the Reconstruction experiment, captured the turbulent spirit of the times in a harsh passage written in 1879:[3]

Of the slain there were enough to furnish forth a battlefield and all from those three classes, the negro, the scalawag, and the carpetbagger—all killed with deliberation, overwhelmed by numbers, roused from slumber at the murk midnight, in the hall of public assembly, upon the river-brink, on the lonely woods-road . . . shot, stabbed, hanged, drowned, mutilated beyond description, tortured beyond conception.

Even after allowances are made for poetic license, there remains a considerable degree of truth in Tourgee's assertion, for the South during Reconstruction was indeed the stage for an almost incredible drama of violence.

One of the most sinister yet interesting struggles of this uneasy period resulted from the organization of Negro militia forces in the Southern states. These forces were created by the Radicals in an attempt to fill the power vacuum that resulted from the withdrawal of Federal troops when the states had complied with the conditions set forth in the Reconstruction acts. The need for the militia grew out of the stern dictates of political self-preservation; in the Radical plan for a Republican South the militia forces were assigned the task of perpetuating the existence of the newly created Republican state governments. However, the Radicals knew that as a prerequisite to the formation of any effective force of their own they must first destroy any existing armed counterforces in the South. Consequently, they made the provisional militia their target. This militia had been created by the provisional governors in the days immediately after Appomattox in an effort to combat the evils that accompanied the paralysis

[3] Albion W. Tourgee, *A Fool's Errand*, p. 246.

of local government, and opposition to it was formidable. Carl Schurz, while on his Southern tour in 1865, telegraphed a vigorous protest to Washington against arming a militia. His view was supported by America's foremost soldier, not yet turned politician, who argued that it would indeed be unwise to arm Southern militia so soon after the war.[4] Federal commanders stationed in the South joined unanimously in bitter condemnation of the scheme. Yet in spite of such distinguished opposition, provisional governors were granted permission to organize militia forces to apprehend criminals, suppress crime, and protect the inhabitants.

Once organized, these militia forces pursued a course of action that made them extremely vulnerable when the Radical attack upon them was launched. Membership was restricted exclusively to whites and was composed primarily of former rebel soldiers, who persisted in wearing their Confederate gray.[5] Their activities were frankly terroristic and were aimed directly at Negroes who displayed a tendency to assert their newly granted independence. Disarming the freedmen was apparently considered a primary duty and one that was fulfilled with relish, according to this excerpt from a letter: "The militia of this county have seized every gun and pistol found in the hands of (so-called) freedmen of this section of the county. They claim that the Statute Laws of Mississippi do not recognize the Negro as having any right to carry arms."[6] In spite of frequent warnings to militia commanders not to

---

[4] William B. Hesseltine, *U. S. Grant, Politician*, p. 69.

[5] John T. Trowbridge, *A Picture of the Desolated States and the Work of Restoration, 1865–1868*, p. 408. (Hereafter cited as *Desolated States*.)

[6] Letter dated December 2, 1865, cited in *Harper's Weekly*, January 13, 1866.

take the law into their own hands, freedmen continued to be assaulted and were often killed, sometimes on private account. The repeated acts of violence forced many governors to disband or otherwise curtail the activities of their militia[7] and, when properly publicized, greatly aided the Radicals in their campaign to popularize the idea that the provisional militia forces had been organized for "the distinct purpose of enforcing the authority of the whites over the blacks."[8]

Consequently, the Radicals were able to abolish the provisional militia with comparative ease. On March 2, 1867, the same day the first Reconstruction Act was passed, an obscure rider attached to the annual Appropriation Act for the Army ordered the disbandment of all militia forces in the Southern states and prohibited the "further organization, arming, or calling into service of the said militia forces, or any part thereof" until so authorized by Congress.[9] In order to obtain necessary funds for the Army, President Johnson felt compelled to sign the bill, but he immediately forwarded to Congress a communication calling attention to the clause prohibiting certain states from employing their militia and lodged a strong protest against the unconstitutionality of such action.[10]

As state governments were reorganized under provisions of the Reconstruction acts, the heretofore suspected need for a protective force became an urgent fact. This was true largely because of the sullen attitude of the prevail-

[7] Trowbridge, *Desolated States*, p. 374.
[8] S. Exec. Doc. 2, 39th Cong., 1st Sess., p. 36.
[9] *Congressional Globe*, 39th Cong., 2d Sess., p. 217.
[10] James D. Richardson, ed., *A Compilation of the Messages and Papers of the Presidents, 1789–1907*, Vol. VI, p. 472. (Hereafter cited as *Messages of the Presidents*.)

ing number of Southern whites who felt that the reorganized governments were based on a calculated policy of disfranchisement-enfranchisement and were little more than artificial creations imposed from without. It soon became obvious that the new administrations existed precariously amid the undisguised hostility of a potentially destructive local opposition.

Agitation for the restoration of militia privileges in the Southern states thus grew directly out of a need to avoid political annihilation of the Radical state governments at the hands of the enemy within. In early 1868, the incoming mail of congressional Radicals contained many requests for legislation to authorize the re-formation of militia units in Southern states. Two points were consistently emphasized in this correspondence: the need for protection and the need for haste in making that protection available. In answer to these appeals, Senate Bill 648 was reported on July 25, 1868, proposing repeal of the law that prohibited the use of militia in the states lately in rebellion.[11]

The introduction of this bill precipitated an acrimonious debate. The anti-Radical group assumed the offensive in condemning the proposition as an invitation to "confusion, disorder, revolution, anarchy, violence, and bloodshed." Political reasons were said to be the motivating power behind the bill. The original prohibition was condemned as a move deliberately intended to weaken non-Republican governments in the South, and the proposed extension of force to the now-sympathetic regimes was denounced.[12] The bitterest attack of all came from Thomas A. Hendricks, of Indiana:[13]

[11] *Congressional Globe*, 40th Cong., 2d Sess., p. 4467.
[12] *Ibid.*, 40th Cong., 3d Sess., p. 84. Senator Charles R. Buckalew, of Pennsylvania, was the spearhead of this attack on the Radicals.
[13] *Ibid.*, p. 82.

The only necessity in these southern states for the maintenance of a large military force results from the fact that you have attempted to reverse the American doctrine and to declare that by force the power of the states shall be placed in the hands of the minority, stripping classes of the right to participation in the government, and then by force governing them.

Radical supporters of the bill quickly moved to its defense. They insisted that the purpose of the militia was to preserve peace rather than to make war. They argued that lawlessness in the Southern states was due to the inability of civil governments to quell disturbances, and senators were warned that "unless we bring about a condition of things in which there is a power lodged with somebody to repress by force the violence that takes place there continually, we shall see no end of the troubles of which we have heard so much for the last year."[14] Senator William Pitt Fessenden, an ardent advocate of the militia, asserted that the only cure for the continued outbreaks in the South was "force, to be exercised by men who dare to exercise it."[15] When B. F. Rice, of Arkansas, promised that if his state was allowed a militia there would no longer be any need for a single federal soldier to be stationed there, he gained considerable support from those becoming increasingly concerned about the nation's expenditures.

From this verbal encounter the Radicals emerged victorious. Exactly two years and a day after the original prohibition was enacted, a law was passed repealing "so much of the act . . . as prohibits the organization, arming, or calling into service of the militia forces of the states of North Carolina, South Carolina, Florida, Alabama, Louisiana and Arkansas."[16] No mention was made of Virginia, Texas, Mississippi, or Georgia because of the insecurity of

[14] *Ibid.*, p. 81.   [15] *Ibid.*, p. 82.   [16] *Ibid.*, p. 325.

the Radical position in those states. The conservative Virginians had not yet accepted their proposed constitution. The Texas constitutional convention had not completed its task, and the social unrest in the state in 1868 was reflected by a fierce wave of Ku Klux Klan activity. Mississippians had rejected outright the constitution of 1868, which had been drawn up by the highly publicized "Black and Tan Convention," and Georgia was in national disfavor for her intemperate action in having arbitrarily unseated many of the Negro legislators whom the costly machinery of the Reconstruction acts had so laboriously aided in electing. Not until July 15, 1870, when these four states appeared to be safely in the Radical fold, were they authorized to organize militia forces.[17]

Acting either illegally in advance of repeal or upon the legal basis when provided, state governments organized and armed their respective militias, which were then launched upon a curious career that included guerrilla campaigns, naval engagements, diplomatic complications, and even full-scale pitched battles complete with artillery, cavalry, and deployment of troops.

Before we enter into the narrative of the Negro militia movement, three fundamental facts must be emphasized in order to place the subject in proper perspective. In the first place, the militia was not the only instrument used by the Radicals in the South; second, militia forces were not active in all Southern states; and third, the militia units were not made up exclusively of Negro troops.

---

[17] *Ibid.*, 41st Cong., 2d Sess., p. 738. By this time, the ultra-Radical Edmund J. Davis was firmly in the saddle in Texas. Mississippi had accepted a revised constitution, and the able scalawag James L. Alcorn had been elected governor. Virginia had accepted a compromise constitution, and Georgia had been brought to heel by the purges of General Alfred H. Terry.

It should be remembered that the militia forces were only one of several instruments used by the Radicals to advance their Southern program. Two others were employed that furnish interesting parallels to the militia: the Freedmen's Bureau and the Union League, or Loyal League. It is unquestionably true that the Freedmen's Bureau rendered a genuine service to the freedman and that the Loyal Leagues that mushroomed over the South furnished him with a political indoctrination he otherwise would not have received. It is also unquestionably true that these two agencies shared with the militia the implacable hostility of the Southern conservatives. The deep-rooted convictions of many Southerners were facetiously yet accurately expressed in the following anecdote by Representative A. H. Ward, of Kentucky, regarding a cartoon he had once seen: [18]

It was a picture of an old lady flourishing a broomstick over the head of her husband with a Negro in the background holding a dog by the neck and flourishing an uplifted lash, with these words issuing from the lips of the darkey:

"Missus whips Massa, Massa licks me, and so you infernal dog, I gib you de debbil."

Congress backs the Freedmen's Bureau, the Bureau backs the darkey, and the Negro gives the white man the devil.

The Union League was perhaps more intensely disliked than the Freedmen's Bureau. Its clandestine meetings and mysterious initiation rites, shrouded in secrecy, led to the wildest speculation and gave rise to all sorts of groundless fears on the part of the whites. When in 1877 a disappointed Negro Republican wrote the following exaggerated account of a league meeting, he only confirmed

[18] *Ibid.*, 39th Cong., 2d Sess., p. 62. Speech delivered in the House of Representatives on January 19, 1867.

the long-standing suspicions of many Southern whites:[19]

It was in these secret meetings that the fabulous tales of forty acres and a mule originated, and confiscation ideas made some of the leading subjects for discussion. Lands were apportioned by imagination, and fine rebel mansions seized by hope. Gentlemen of African descent saw themselves rearbacked with all the pomp and dignity of princes in their old masters' carriages. . . . Civil rights bills were to be passed by Congress, that would allow them to occupy front seats in white churches, sit at the same table with their former masters, and be respected with all the modern civilities in their parlors and drawing rooms.

The Freedmen's Bureau and the Union League were similar to the militia in that they exacerbated already strained feelings and were directly associated with much of the violence that occurred during the period.

It is also necessary to understand that militia forces were not created and employed in all the Southern states. Staid old Virginia, for example, never organized a Negro militia. Her politicians, acting through a committee of nine, worked out a compromise with the Radicals in Washington concerning the constitution of 1868 that solved most of the pressing political problems. The Gilbert C. Walker administration, elected in July, 1869, was the result of a fusion of Democrats and Conservative Republicans; and since there was no truly Radical government in Virginia, no protective militia force was necessary.

More surprising was the fact that the usually obstreperous state of Georgia also had no regularly organized militia forces. The conservative element was always fairly well represented in Georgia affairs, even during the Bul-

[19] John T. Shuften, *A Colored Man's Exposition of the Acts and Doings of the Republican Party South*, p. 8.

lock administration. Too, the powerful personal influence of former Governor Joseph E. Brown, who consistently pleaded for moderation, was a potent force on the local scene. More important than anything else, perhaps, was the fact that throughout the entire period the Democrats maintained their hold on the county offices, thereby preventing the development of a conspicuously successful Radical government in the state.[20]

In Alabama, Governor William H. Smith, who held office as an appointee of General George Gordon Meade, had elaborate paper plans for a militia system but consistently refused to arm any troops. At the height of Ku Klux Klan depredations in that state, he threatened to call out Negro troops to suppress lawlessness, but no such order was ever issued. Three years later, his successor ordered the adjutant general not to enroll Negro militia even in the face of a determined White League movement aimed at the eventual destruction of his regime. When Alabama Republicans split in 1874, the "bolters" organized squads of Negro troops who were known as "National Guards" but were not genuine state militia.[21]

The situation in Florida was quite similar to that in Alabama. After the inauguration of Harrison Reed in June, 1868, Negro troops were organized and armed. But in spite of the numerous outbreaks of violence that marked his administration, Reed steadfastly refused to use his militia for fear of starting a race war. As a general rule, Reed was satisfied to allow federal troops to settle any difficulties that arose.

[20] Mildred Thompson, *Reconstruction in Georgia*, p. 365.
[21] Walter L. Fleming, *Civil War and Reconstruction in Alabama*, p. 774.

In the remaining states, Negro troops were organized and actually employed in varying degrees. In Tennessee, with its own peculiar Reconstruction history, troops were organized by Governor William G. Brownlow early in 1867. His militia did not actually fight any pitched battles but were employed primarily in political assignments, where they proved themselves more annoying than overpowering. They were mustered in on several occasions as anti–Ku Klux Klan forces but were never really effective on a state-wide basis.

Arkansas was one of the most active of the Southern states in the Negro militia movement. Negro troops were organized and armed after the inauguration of Governor Powell Clayton in July, 1868. The first great wave of militia activity came in late 1868 and early 1869, when Clayton proclaimed martial law, as a result of which his troops marched and countermarched over the state for four months. The second wave occurred during April and May of 1874, when the forces of rival claimants for the governorship fought a fair-sized war for control of the state government.

The Negro militia in Texas was intimately associated with the political career of Governor Edmund J. Davis. This official used his troops freely during the election of 1871 and also called them out to enforce declarations of martial law in several counties during the same period. When Davis was defeated by Judge Richard Coke in the gubernatorial election in December, 1873, there ensued a struggle between Coke's supporters and Davis' Negro troops for possession of the Statehouse in Austin.

In Louisiana, Negro troops were first organized by Governor Henry C. Warmoth in June, 1870, and placed under the command of Lee's renowned war horse, General James Longstreet. From that time until the final Packard-Nicholls struggle ending in 1877, the troops were used on various occasions. In 1872, when the Carter-Warmoth feud split the party in Louisiana, troops were called out to protect Republicans from other Republicans. The troops were used again in 1873, during the Kellogg-McEnery contest, and in September, 1874, they fought a pitched battle in the barricaded streets of New Orleans against the White League.

In Mississippi, the militia issue remained quiescent during the early years of Radical rule. Following the inauguration of James L. Alcorn as governor in 1870, militia units were organized in a desultory manner. Alcorn apparently never shed enough of his ingrained conservatism to become a full-fledged Radical; and by 1871, when he resigned the governorship to go to the Senate, no Negro troops had actually been used in Mississippi. However, after the Republican faction headed by Adelbert Ames won out in the struggle for party leadership, the tempo of violence increased throughout the state. In 1874 and 1875, riot followed riot. Finally, in the harsh afterlight of the Clinton slaughter, Ames decided to place his militia on a war footing, and a period of feverish preparations followed. A crisis was avoided by the negotiation of a compromise in mid-October, 1875, when the so-called "Peace Agreement" was signed in Jackson by the belligerents.

North Carolina suffered only one spasm of violence connected with the militia. W. W. Holden, elected governor in 1868, first called up his troops to cope with Ku Klux Klan disturbances. In June, 1870, he placed his troops under the command of George W. Kirk, former Colonel of

United States Volunteers and a native of Tennessee, and for a period of six months the state was involved in either physical or legal phases of the fight that has gone down in the history books as the Kirk-Holden War.

After Arkansas, South Carolina was the most active of the Southern states in the Negro militia movement. Robert K. Scott, the first of the South Carolina Radical governors, armed the Negro troops just before the campaign that resulted in his re-election in 1870. For several years thereafter, the Ku Klux Klan and the militia engaged in a vendetta that ended only when President Grant ordered nine counties of the state placed under martial law and sent United States troops to enforce his proclamation. Franklin J. Moses, Jr., who succeeded Scott as governor, continued the policy of his predecessor in regard to the use of Negro troops, as did his successor, Daniel H. Chamberlain, with only minor variations. The victims of the massacre at Hamburg were members of a Negro militia company, and lesser conflicts claimed the lives of many more until the accession of Wade Hampton in 1877.

The third fact that should be understood about the so-called "Negro militia" is that it was not composed entirely of Negroes. Varying numbers of whites belonged to the militia units in every state. In Arkansas, South Carolina, Mississippi, and Texas, there were heavy concentrations of Negro troops, and there was a noticeable mixture of Negro and white troops in the Tennessee, Louisiana, and North Carolina companies. The militia was nevertheless considered a "Negro militia," in keeping with the long-standing Southern indifference to logic when considering questions involving race. As in heredity, so in the militia, a touch of Negro was sufficient to brand it as all Negro in the eyes of most Southern whites. The feeling of resent-ment that resulted from placing armed Negroes in positions of authority over Southern whites goes a long way toward explaining the violent reaction that inevitably accompanied militia activities.

II. Organizing and Arming the Militia

ONCE THE LEGAL GROUNDWORK had been prepared by Congress, local Radicals, reacting to the increasing pressure of Conservative opposition, speedily assumed the offensive in organizing their state militia forces. Although the procedure differed in detail from state to state, the organizational technique that was employed followed a fairly definite pattern. First came careful cultivation of favorable public opinion. This was followed by well-timed gubernatorial appeals to state legislatures that led directly to passage of militia laws.

In order to gain public support for creation of the militia, campaigns were inaugurated to emphasize the desperate need for such forces. Incumbent Radical governors were voluble spokesmen in support of the plan. Time and again they cried out against the lack of any real force with which to quell disturbances, while continuing to point out the extremely violent nature of their opposition. R. K. Scott, of South Carolina, speaking in the District of Columbia just before the state election of 1870, informed his audience that the only law South Carolinians really understood was the Winchester rifle.[1] Brownlow, while stumping Tennessee in behalf of his own candidacy, pleaded with the voters also to "send up a legislature to reorganize the militia" and promised to put an end to the violence sweeping over the state if his plea was granted.[2]

Properly publicized reports of legislative investigating committees, emphasizing the general lawlessness of the

[1] Henry T. Thompson, *Ousting the Carpetbagger from South Carolina*, p. 48.

[2] James W. Patton, *Unionism and Reconstruction in Tennessee, 1860–1869*, p. 86 (hereafter cited as *Reconstruction in Tennessee*), citing *Nashville* (Tenn.) *Daily Times*, January 16, 1865.

period, also aided in creating sentiment favorable to the organization of militia. In Texas, for example, the *Report of the Committee on Lawlessness* presented statistics on deaths by violence in the period from the close of the war to June, 1868. Although the figures showed 509 whites had been killed as opposed to 486 freedmen, it was asserted that over 90 per cent of the total number of killings had been committed by whites while little more than 1 per cent of the deaths resulted from attacks by freedmen on whites.[3] A similar committee of the Louisiana Legislature, investigating fraud and violence in that state during the presidential election of 1868, closed its report with the suggestion that "it might be well to inquire whether a small body of mounted militia, which can be moved to any part of the state where it is needed, upon short notice, should not at once be organized."[4]

At the same time, the governors passed up no opportunity to describe the woeful conditions under which they were forced to operate. Governor Davis, of Texas, spoke for all his comrades-in-office when he complained that "the state government is without any militia or police whatever."[5] Governor Brownlow, describing conditions in Tennessee, lamented that "the state arms were carried into the rebellion through the influence of the bad men in authority four years ago, and throughout the length and breadth of the state, she has not arms enough to arm a captain's company."[6]

---

[3] This report was published in the *Journal of the Convention of 1868* and is cited in Charles W. Ramsdell, *Reconstruction in Texas*, p. 219.

[4] *Report of the Joint Committee of the Louisiana Legislature on the Election of 1868*, p. xxxix.

[5] S. Misc. Doc. 109, 40th Cong., 2d Sess., p. 6.

[6] *Acts of the State of Tennessee, 1865*, p. 6.

Considerable public support was generated for the militia movement as a result of these public utterances. When local political barometers indicated the propitious moment, governors then issued official appeals to their respective legislatures. Citing the obvious shortcomings of the existing situation, they urged immediate and effective remedies. Yet they couched their appeals in very cautious language and gave repeated assurances that if granted militia forces they would call them out only in cases of general resistance to the laws. Although the desired result was uniform throughout the Southern states, gubernatorial requests were quite different in nature. Where the Texas Legislature was merely urged to "look into the question" of making some provision for the temporary establishment of martial law,[7] Governor Clayton peremptorily demanded that the Arkansas Legislature, in the interests of public safety, must "proceed at once to provide for an efficient and well disciplined militia."[8] Governor Holden, in his message to the North Carolina lawmakers, virtually pleaded with them to enact laws that would enable him "to suppress violence and disorder"[9] and piously added that such action would allow his administration to appear equipped with both "the olive branch and the sword."[10] Governor Brownlow characteristically promised that if given a militia force he would bring peace to Tennessee if he had "to shoot and hang every man concerned."[11]

On the basis of these appeals, state legislators set about

[7] Hilary A. Herbert, ed., *Why the Solid South?* p. 371.

[8] Powell Clayton, *The Aftermath of the Civil War in Arkansas,* p. 41. (Hereafter cited as *Aftermath in Arkansas.*)

[9] William W. Holden, *Memoirs,* p. 121.

[10] James G. de R. Hamilton, *Reconstruction in North Carolina,* p. 401.

[11] Patton, *Reconstruction in Tennessee,* p. 86, citing *Nashville* (Tenn.) *Daily Times,* January 16, 1865.

the task of drafting and enacting militia laws. When completed, these laws authorized creation of military forces that were patterned largely after the United States Army and were, in the main, subject to rules quite similar to the Articles of War. Although varying in detail, the laws fundamentally had much in common. In general, they provided for a force made up of two components, a state guard and a reserve militia. The regular, or active-duty, personnel belonged to the guard, while the reserve militia furnished a reservoir of manpower for necessary mobilization. The number of troops authorized varied from state to state. Some states (for example, North Carolina) were quite specific about the maximum number that could be enrolled,[12] while others left the decision entirely to the discretion of the governor.[13] Usually the eligible age group was eighteen to forty-five years. The governor was ex officio commander-in-chief of the state forces and had explicit power to call out the militia whenever in his opinion circumstances warranted such action. He was further empowered to assess and collect taxes from troublesome counties in order to defray costs of militia operations therein. His personal grip on the militia was assured because he had complete control of the selection of officers. Exemption clauses, under which less belligerent members of the community might avoid military service in return for payment of an annual tax to the military fund, were frequently included in the militia laws. The tax ranged from

[12] The militia bill passed in North Carolina in 1868 prohibited the enrollment of more than 6,000 men. See Hamilton, *Reconstruction in North Carolina*, p. 358.

[13] The wording of the South Carolina militia law passed in 1868 authorized the governor to "employ as many persons as he may deem necessary and proper for the suppression of insurrection, rebellion, or resistance to the laws." (James S. Reynolds, *Reconstruction in South Carolina*, p. 114.)

as little as two dollars in North Carolina to much higher figures in other states.[14] North Carolina also provided an exemption from service for anyone who was excused by written authority of a competent physician.[15] Only two states seem to have recognized that some citizens rendered things other than to Caesar. Any North Carolinian imbued with peace-loving "religious scruples" was constitutitionally excused from performing militia duty,[16] and professed conscientious objectors in Arkansas were excluded from involuntary service by a specific clause written into the law.[17]

Several of the laws contained provisions that, although peculiar to the state concerned, throw additional light on the militia forces as they were eventually organized. In Mississippi, for instance, militiamen were immune from arrest while attending or going to and from musters.[18] A clause in the North Carolina law called for separation of the races into different companies.[19] The South Carolina law contained two unusual provisions. The first, reflecting a sound insight into the military importance of transport and communication, authorized the governor to take possession of telegraph and railroads in times of emergency, and the second imposed both fine and imprisonment as penalties against bodies other than the militia for organizing, drilling, or parading anywhere in the state.[20]

[14] For figures on North Carolina, see Hamilton, *Reconstruction in North Carolina*, p. 358. In Arkansas, the annual tax was five dollars. (Thomas S. Staples, *Reconstruction in Arkansas*, p. 289.)

[15] Hamilton, *Reconstruction in North Carolina*, p. 358.

[16] Specifically stated in the constitution of North Carolina drawn up in 1868.

[17] Arkansas constitution of 1868, Art. XI, Sec. 1.

[18] *Journal of the Proceedings in the Constitutional Convention of the State of Mississippi, 1868*, p. 641. This provision was included in the Mississippi constitution of 1868, Art. IX, Sec. 8.

[19] Hamilton, *Reconstruction in North Carolina*, p. 359.

[20] Reynolds, *Reconstruction in South Carolina*, pp. 115, 119.

Acting on these laws, Radical governors began organizing their militia forces. Although enrollment was legally open to both races, it soon became apparent that most of the volunteers would be Negroes. This should not have been surprising. Many whites were officially discouraged from joining because of justifiable Radical suspicions concerning their intent. On the other hand, Negroes had ample reason to be devoted to the Republican cause.

The Conservatives made a deliberate attempt to organize and receive arms under provisions of the militia laws. This infiltration was encouraged by their political leaders, who could foresee the real advantage inherent in having their personal supporters armed at the expense of the state.[21] This attempted wolf-in-sheep's-clothing maneuver was foiled, however. Opposition to the inclusion of Conservatives in the militia was spearheaded by loyal troops already mustered in. North Carolina's Governor Holden was warned against the possibility of Conservatives gaining control of the militia by being the first to offer their services "under the pretence that they are 'alright' and ancious to put down the depradations that [are] now being perpetrated in this state."[22] Many protests were heard from organized units:[23]

The present companies that have already been armed and equipped are loyal, peacable, orderly, and efficient, and can be controlled for the good of the country. They are insenced over

[21] General J. Z. George, for example, consistently urged Mississippi Democrats to enroll in the militia. (James W. Garner, *Reconstruction in Mississippi*, p. 383.)

[22] I. C. Williams to William W. Holden, June 28, 1870, William W. Holden Papers.

[23] Letter from B. G. Yocum dated September 2, 1870, published in *Report of Joint Investigating Committee on Public Frauds in South Carolina, 1877–1878*, p. 674. Yocum was a colonel in the Fourteenth Regiment of South Carolina Militia.

the prospect of having an armed and authorized enemy to contend against, and say if the Governor is going to arm the white KK's to operate against them, he, the Governor, can take back the guns and commissions that has already been sent to this county. . . . It will not be so funny if our best men get killed off by those villins. . . .

One militiaman penned his fervent hope that no Conservative would be allowed to enroll, "for if they git controle of the state troots in the different counties as the secessionists did after the surrender (at the close of the war) of the county police our generals may be ever so vigerlent but they will make but little success in putting down the outrages." He closed his letter with a warning to put "none on garde tonight but loyal citizens."[24]

Radical governors, taking their lead from the expressed resentment of their own supporters, moved to exclude Conservatives from the militia. In Louisiana, it was demanded that "men should prove they are loyal before they can be trusted to go into the militia."[25] The Alabama ordinance provided that commissions in the state militia would be reserved for "persons of known loyalty."[26] Governor Ames, of Mississippi, made the realistic observation that, since "the state government commanded the respect of the colored race only, it must depend for military support on colored troops."[27] In areas where white companies of questionable loyalty had been allowed to organize, disbandment, when considered necessary, was easily effected by the expedient of appointing Negro

[24] I. C. Williams to William W. Holden, June 28, 1870, Holden Papers.
[25] Ella Lonn, *Reconstruction in Louisiana after 1868*, p. 22. (Hereafter cited as *Reconstruction in Louisiana.*)
[26] *Harper's Weekly*, December 21, 1867.
[27] Garner, *Reconstruction in Mississippi*, p. 385.

officers to positions of command.[28] By these means, white participation in the militia was largely limited to those who had given previous evidence of Republican sympathies.

The Negro, on the other hand, had several positive motives for enlisting in the militia. In the novelty of his freedom, he did not forget the men who had made that freedom possible. Since the Negro was circumstantially a Republican, it was quite natural for him to support party programs. This was particularly true of the militia project, where participation could be interpreted as a personal defense of his freedom. Political affinity was, however, only one of the factors that made the Negro a willing recruit. The pay, normally the same as that received by soldiers of equivalent grade or rank in the United States Army, was enticing. Indeed, to the average field hand, the reward must have appeared magnificent. Too, the perennial appeal of the uniform exercised some influence, especially since regulations were lax enough to allow the sporting of an occasional plume or feather. The promised relief from the routine drudgery of plantation work probably accounted for many more volunteers. The drills, the parades, the barbecues, and the speeches offered a pleasant break in the monotony, and soldiering was considered a delightful game.[29]

Another reason for increased Negro enlistment was social pressure. Negro women, emulating the role played by their white sisters of the South during the Civil War, were very effective recruiters for the militia. Failure to show interest in the movement automatically caused the

[28] Claude G. Bowers, *The Tragic Era*, p. 359; Reynolds, *Reconstruction in South Carolina*, pp. 136–37.
[29] J. A. Leland, *A Voice from South Carolina*, p. 49.

male Negro to become politically suspect and gave rise to a most rigorous program of discrimination at the hands of the women. Negro men charged with political infidelity were socially isolated; they even encountered increasing difficulty in persuading a woman to wash their clothing. Expulsion from the local church was not considered too extreme a punishment, and on several occasions groups of irate females publicly assaulted and tore the clothing off suspected shirkers. In cases involving reluctant husbands, wives were known to impose restraints that certainly must have taxed the domestic relationship.[30] Such efforts were not without results, and under the additional pressure of circulated handbills bearing the appeal "To Arms! To Arms!! To Arms!!! Colored Men to the Front!"[31] the muster lists were rapidly filled.

Hand in hand with the actual formation of militia forces went the problem of officer procurement. Inasmuch as the selection of officers was generally left in the hands of the governor, no uniform system of appointment evolved. One qualification remained fairly constant, however: the appointee must be a person of known loyalty to the cause. During periods of militia activity, governors were overwhelmed by letters from commission-seekers. Some requests—and resulting appointments—were of a strictly political nature, while others were based on ability and experience. The Governor of Tennessee received the following straightforward appeal:[32]

---

[30] This sampling of Negro discrimination against other Negroes is taken from the testimony of the victims. (S. Misc. Doc. 48, Vol. I, 44th Cong., 2d Sess., pp. 556, 560, *et passim.*)

[31] Cited in H.R. Misc. Doc. 211. 42d Cong., 2d Sess., p. 319.

[32] N. C. Davis to William G. Brownlow, May 18, 1867, William G. Brownlow Papers.

In the Name and by the Authority of

The State of Texas.

Know Ye, That I, EDMUND J. DAVIS, *Governor of the State of Texas, reposing special trust and confidence in the patriotism, valor, fidelity and ability of* J. S. Dick , *do appoint him* Second Lieutenant *in Militia of Texas, to rank as* Such *from the* 3rd *day of* October *One Thousand Eight Hundred and Seventy . He is, therefore, carefully and diligently to discharge the duty of* 2d Lieutenant *by doing and performing all manner of things, thereunto belonging; and I do strictly charge and require all persons under his command to be obedient to his orders, as* 2d Lieutenant *; and he is to observe, and follow such orders and directions, from time to time, as he shall receive from his superior officers, set over him according to the rules and discipline, laid down for the guidance of the Militia forces of this State.*

This commission to continue in force during the pleasure of the Commander-in-Chief, for the time being.

In Testimony Whereof, *I have hereunto signed my name, and caused the Great Seal of the State to be affixed, at the City of Austin, the* 3rd *day of* October *, in the year of our Lord One Thousand Eight Hundred and Seventy , and the Independence of Texas the Thirty* Fifth *.*

Edmund J. Davis
Governor of Texas.

By the Governor:

J. C. Oldright
Act'g Secretary of State.

Recorded: Volume 1 *, page* 252 *,*
Adjutant General's Office,
Austin Oct 3rd 1870

James Davidson
ADJUTANT GENERAL,
State of Texas.

X Edward Beck
Clerk
In charge.

Second Lieutenant's commission, Texas Militia
(Texas State Archives, Austin)

Sir

As I am a man of few words I will tell you at once without any apology or preliminaries what I want. I want a Captain's commission to recruit a company of black soldiers for the state guards. I have served three years in the Federal army and can give the best of references as to character and ability.

In some cases the men were allowed to elect their officers, although this practice was by no means general. Commissions were sometimes placed on the auction block and fell to the highest bidder, and letters such as the following were common: [33]

Hamburg, S. C., June 3, 1876

Mr. Henry B. Johnson:

Sir: Would you be kind enough to see what it would cost me to get the commission for one captain and three lieutenants. If you will see Col. Walter R. Jones and ask him to assist you in getting the commissions for me, and send them to me, and i will return the expensy on the return mail. . . .

Col. John Williams

In order to obtain the services of physicians for the militia, private contracts were negotiated under whose terms medical officers were brought into service with a higher rate of pay than that of the troops. [34]

Having arranged for the organization of militia forces, the authorities were next faced with the problem of arming and equipping them. This proved to be a most difficult task. Militia appropriations were bitterly and often successfully opposed by Conservative blocs, and governors were forced to seek other methods by which to equip their forces. The first such measure was an attempt to

[33] S. Misc. Doc. 48, Vol. III, 44th Cong., 2d Sess., p. 585.
[34] Several copies of these contracts may be found in the files of the Tennessee Adjutant General's Office. (Hereafter cited as AGO files, state of Tennessee.)

borrow guns and ammunition from the armories of sympathetic Northern states. For this purpose Governor Clayton, of Arkansas, sent a personal envoy, Dr. J. M. Lewis, to enter a plea with the governor of Illinois;[35] Warmoth, of Louisiana, sent a representative to the capitals of Missouri and Illinois;[36] while Governor Reed, of Florida, personally called on Governor John Andrew, of Massachusetts, and Governor Reuben Fenton, of New York.[37] Although these appeals generally fell on deaf ears, Vermont, in answer to an appeal from the adjutant general of North Carolina, sent 1,000 Springfield rifles to aid in pacifying the citizenry of that state.[38]

Failing in this effort, the governors next turned to the federal government in hopes of securing arms for their troops. Their earliest overtures met with official rebuff. Clayton's request for arms was denied by the Army,[39] as was a similar plea from the Governor of Florida.[40] However, as violence in the Southern states continued unabated, the national administration gradually began to look with more favor on the possibility of furnishing arms to state governments. Apparently the adjutant general of South Carolina was the first to persuade the federal government to make an issue of arms to a state, for his opponents at home reported with noticeable chagrin: "He CAME to Washington, he SAW the Secretary, he CONQUERED all objections."[41] When Governor Holden, of North Carolina, sought federal aid in outfitting his troops, he re-

[35] Clayton, *Aftermath in Arkansas*, pp. 106–109.
[36] H.R. Misc. Doc. 154, 42d Cong., 2d Sess., p. 519.
[37] John Wallace, *Carpetbag Rule in Florida*, p. 92.
[38] Hamilton, *Reconstruction in North Carolina*, p. 346.
[39] Clayton, *Aftermath in Arkansas*, pp. 106–109.
[40] Wallace, *Carpetbag Rule in Florida*, p. 92.
[41] *Proceedings of the Tax-Payer's Convention of South Carolina, 1874*, p. 95.

ceived support from no less powerful a person than President Grant. Holden sent a political associate, William G. Clarke, to Washington as his agent. Clarke, on his arrival, wrote a formal request to General Montgomery C. Meigs, Quartermaster General of the Army, for equipment to outfit a full regiment of North Carolina infantry.[42] Clarke then secured a personal interview with Grant during which he gained the President's approval of the project. On the same day Grant wrote a letter to General Sherman endorsing the plan to outfit North Carolina troops at government expense and said that he was "willing to sign any legal order necessary" to accomplish it.[43] Sherman then agreed to issue the equipment in exchange for Governor Holden's signature on a bond that would be "payable at the day of Judgment."[44] Several days later, Holden was informed by Meigs that the quartermaster at Fortress Monroe had been instructed to issue the outfit.[45]

Eventually, Congress passed a law authorizing the distribution of federal arms to Southern states on a quota basis.[46] In practice, this system proved quite flexible. Governor Scott, for example, persuaded the authorities to issue South Carolina a sizable advance on its quota.[47] It is not too broad a generalization to say that this law pro-

[42] William G. Clarke to Montgomery C. Meigs, June 17, 1870, Holden Papers.

[43] Ulysses S. Grant to William T. Sherman, June 17, 1870, Holden Papers.

[44] William G. Clarke to William W. Holden, June 18, 1870, Holden Papers.

[45] Montgomery C. Meigs to William W. Holden, June 21, 1870, Holden Papers.

[46] Act of March 3, 1873. See *Congressional Globe*, 42d Cong., 3d Sess., p. 300.

[47] B. R. Tillman, *The Struggles of '76*, p. 40 (pamphlet in the possession of the author). Tillman, in a highly partisan vein, estimates that Scott received a twenty-year allotment in advance.

vided the largest single source of arms and equipment for the various state militias.[48]

Since the organization and arming of the militia was not carried out in secrecy, it was accompanied by vociferous opposition from the Conservatives. Every news organ at their disposal carried on a vituperative campaign against the militia project, denouncing it as a flagrant encroachment on civil liberties. Editorials similar to the following appeared frequently:[49]

The whole affair is a weak and silly attempt to awaken the worst passions of the aggressive party with a view to make them a unit in support of executive violence, and to browbeat and intimidate. . . . He [Governor Clayton] wants 23,000 negroes armed to protect 70,000 white men and their families in order to promote future peace, quiet and permanency.

When militia bills were introduced in state legislatures, prominent Democrats led the fight against them.[50] The proposed laws were attacked as purely political in nature and as potential threats to the preservation of peace.[51] Nor was opposition confined to the South. As influential a newspaper as James Gordon Bennett's *New York Herald* matched and often outdistanced the provincial Southern press in rabid denunciation: "The fact is inevitable that bloodshed will follow. Reconstructed governments are bad

[48] For detailed information concerning federal issue of arms to Southern states from 1865 to 1872, see official figures cited in H.R. Misc. Doc. 191, 42d Cong., 2d Sess., p. 4.

[49] *Daily Arkansas Gazette*, November 26, 1868.

[50] Testimony of Plato Durham, H.R. Rep. 22, 42d Cong., 2d Sess., p. 317.

[51] A Louisiana senator stated flatly, "I believe the object of the bill, as it stands, is to perpetuate the power of . . . the Republican Party." (Cited in Lonn, *Reconstruction in Louisiana*, p. 60.) Democrats repeatedly warned that if militia bills were passed it would become impossible to preserve peace. (Testimony of H. C. Warmoth, H.R. Misc. Doc., 154, 42d Cong., 2d Sess., p. 519.)

enough with negro legislators, negro magistrates, negro police, and negro Commissioners of Education and other matters; but when armed negroes appear as military forces to keep white men in order . . . the spirit . . . must revolt."[52] When recruiting actually began, Conservatives loudly claimed they were being discriminated against in not being allowed to join up. They cited the difficulties put in the way to prevent their enlisting as clear evidence of official preference for Negro troops.[53] They tossed in an incidental complaint that recruiting among agricultural workers interfered with the harvesting of crops.[54] Great excitement prevailed over the question of arming the militia. In an attempt to prevent passage of a proposed act allowing the federal government to issue arms to Southern governors, Representative Nathaniel Boyden, of North Carolina, made this impassioned plea: "Great God, we cannot afford to fight each other. . . . I warn the House that if arms are sent there, we will be ruined; we cannot live there. If we need anything in the way of arms, in God's name send an army of the United States but do not arm neighbor against neighbor."[55] Loud protests were registered when rifles were issued for drill purposes; and when live ammunition was subsequently passed out, consternation reigned. The Conservatives maintained that conflict was inevitable after the "buck and ball" reached the hands of militiamen.[56]

The governors were not intimidated by the clamorings

[52] *New York Herald,* October 1, 1868.

[53] Garner, *Reconstruction in Mississippi,* p. 383.

[54] —. —. Stuart to Governor William G. Brownlow, April 1, 1867, Brownlow Papers.

[55] Hamilton, *Reconstruction in North Carolina,* p. 372, citing a speech made in the House of Representatives in August, 1868.

[56] Testimony of David R. Duncan, H.R. Rep. 22, Vol. II, Part 3, 42d Cong., 2d Sess., p. 880.

and threats of their political antagonists. They defended their action on the firm grounds that the right of a state to organize a militia was not a new principle but a very old one and that it was designed not to foment trouble but to preserve peace. In a speech at Lewisburg, Arkansas, at the very height of the militia-organization controversy in 1868, Governor Clayton courageously said: "I understand that the militia law is distasteful to some. I have only to say that it is a law that will be enforced. The militia forces will be organized in this county and throughout the state."[57]

The governors were not without support. Letters from all sections of their states poured into the capitals in praise of the militia movement. This correspondence demonstrated a widespread interest in the organization of the militia and the desire to see that it was made "both ornamental and useful."[58] In South Carolina, it was reported that "the colored people are rejoicing over their guns."[59] Governor Davis received this gratifying message from a fellow-Texan: "All the Union mens of this county is proud of the militia and Police law and hopes you will inforce them. We have many roughies here should be tried by the military."[60]

Out of the welter of accusations, exaggerations, recriminations, charges, and countercharges that resulted from the organization of militia forces, a few reasonable con-

[57] Clayton, *Aftermath in Arkansas*, p. 148.
[58] G. R. Dickson to William W. Holden, April 5, 1870, Holden Papers.
[59] Letter from J. A. Jackson to John B. Hubbard, July 3, 1870, quoted in *Report of Joint Investigating Committee on Public Frauds in South Carolina, 1877–1878*, p. 675.
[60] Undated letter of A. P. Brown to Edmund J. Davis, quoted in J. M. Brewer, *Negro Legislators of Texas*, p. 58. Brown was a Negro politician of Hopkins County.

clusions may be made. Certainly, the need for a protective force was a very real one, if the Radicals were to maintain their hold on Southern state governments. Their resolute action in forming militia units was an accurate indication of their political sagacity. Also, it does not seem likely that there was any deliberate attempt, except in a few isolated instances, to make this force exclusively Negro. That it became so was probably a great surprise to the originators, many of whom lacked the familiarity with Southern attitudes and behavior that usually comes only from long observation of sectional peculiarities. It is also true that in spite of an unfavorable publicity campaign of unprecedented proportions, the Radicals persevered in the work of arming their forces.

Once this was accomplished, the stage was set for the enactment of a drama of violence that was to last until the final disintegration of the Radical dream of a Republican South.

III. The Militia in Action

TOWARD THE END of January, 1889, twelve years after the dissolution of the last Negro militia unit in the South, there occurred a brutal murder in Conway County, Arkansas. This crime is of particular interest because the murdered man was John M. Clayton, brother of the Radical Governor who organized and employed Negro troops in that state. During the investigation that followed the murder it was rumored that Clayton had been killed by Thomas Hooper, then a citizen of California, in revenge for the killing of his father by Clayton's militia during the hectic days of 1868.[1] Whether or not the rumor was true is largely beside the point in so far as this book is concerned, but it is certainly indicative of the fact that during the period of militia activity seeds of ill-feeling were sown that were to yield fruits of hatred for many years to come.

Since much of this ill-feeling resulted directly from deeds involving Negro militia forces, it is necessary to analyze their activities in order to arrive at some acceptable picture of their history. In attempting such an analysis, one must avoid the extreme positions reflected not only in the uniform denunciations of those who opposed the militia but also in the unparalleled praise of its advocates. Historians of the Reconstruction period offer little aid here, since their accounts of the militia in action vary almost as widely as did contemporary ones. Dunningites, for example, persistently portray the militiamen as arrogant, swaggering bullies bent on a rapacious campaign of violence against and humiliation of the South. Revisionists, on the other hand, when they mention the militia

[1] For full account see Clayton, *Aftermath in Arkansas*, p. 191.

at all, tend to describe their activities as little more than a series of playful pranks committed by a troupe of benevolent comics.[2] As is so often the case when differing schools of thought assume such remote positions, the truth lies somewhere in between. In this case, Negro militia units were neither so evil an influence as their Conservative opponents claimed nor so saintly as their Radical defenders asserted. A more balanced view is that militiamen were not nearly so vicious as they were painted by their enemies but that they did from time to time become involved in activities that contributed to the deterioration of relations and led almost inevitably to outbreaks of violence.

By far the greatest area of activity for the militia forces was in the realm of politics. Throughout their career they were a factor in local political strategy. The timing involved in organizing these forces strongly suggests political motivation. In Tennessee, for example, Governor Brownlow mobilized troops just before the election in which he defeated Emerson Etheridge for the governorship.[3] In Arkansas, Clayton called up his forces in September, 1868, one month before the general election of that year.[4] Governor Ames, of Mississippi, put his Negro units on a war footing during the heated campaign of 1875 in that state.[5] The Kirk forces were enrolled in North

[2] S. E. Morison and H. S. Commager, in *The Growth of the American Republic* (Vol. II, p. 42), refer to the Negro militia as a "comic force." F. B. Simkins, in *A History of the South* (p. 281), erroneously states that Arkansas, Tennessee, and North Carolina employed no Negro troops in their respective militia forces. He also erroneously concludes that there was little actual violence connected with the militia experiment.

[3] Patton, *Reconstruction in Tennessee*, p. 176. The troops were disbanded immediately after the election.

[4] Clayton, *Aftermath in Arkansas*, p. 63.

[5] S. Rep. 527, 44th Cong., 1st Sess., p. 6.

Carolina during June and July, 1870, just before the scheduled election of August 4;[6] and in South Carolina, Governor Scott armed 20,000 Negro troops before his re-election in 1870.[7] The effectiveness of the militia in politics can be fairly measured by the following survey of results of the presidential election of 1868. Grant and Colfax were the Republican nominees; Seymour and Blair represented the Democrats. In the Southern states, Republicans were victorious directly in proportion to their military preparedness. In Tennessee, Florida, North Carolina, South Carolina, and Arkansas, where militia forces had actually been organized before the election, Grant and Colfax carried the day. In Louisiana and Georgia, where no militia forces had been organized by November, 1868, Seymour and Blair won out. Alabama, where militia laws had been enacted although troops had not actually been enrolled, supported Grant. Mississippi, Texas, and Virginia were not yet reorganized and therefore did not take part in the election.

Militia forces were frequently employed during political campaigns. Nineteen companies were distributed over Tennessee in one pre-election period.[8] Brownlow's opponent in the campaign, when speaking at Franklin, had to contend with a noisy company of Negro militia placed in close proximity to the platform.[9] A prominent South Carolinian complained that during the campaign of 1870

[6] *Raleigh* (N.C.) *Daily Sentinel,* June 22, 1870.

[7] Francis B. Simkins and R. H. Woody, *South Carolina during Reconstruction,* p. 451. See also James Ford Rhodes, *History of the United States from the Compromise of 1850 to Final Restoration of Home Rule at the South in 1877,* Vol. VII, p. 157.

[8] E. Merton Coulter, *William G. Brownlow, Fighting Parson of the Southern Highlands,* pp. 338–39. (Hereafter cited as *Brownlow.*)

[9] *Nashville* (Tenn.) *Union and Dispatch,* July 11, 1867, cited in Patton, *Reconstruction in Tennessee,* p. 177.

almost every public meeting was "attended by the militia of Governor Scott."[10] Any anti-Radical politician was considered fair game for heckling.[11] When one governor informed his troops that he did not consider it their duty "to stand quietly by and hear men excite the mob spirit by denouncing the federal and state governments,"[12] he was in effect authorizing them to interfere in local campaigns, since almost any Democratic political speech could be interpreted as a denouncement of one or the other. Reports from militia detachments show that they were not entirely unaware of their political responsibilities. "We are making every effort to carry the county and can do so,"[13] said one informant, and another categorically promised: "I will carry the election here with the militia. . . . I am giving out ammunition all the time."[14] In Mississippi, pre-election preparations were described in the following letter from Yazoo City:[15]

Mr. Thompson My Dear
friend, it is with Pleasure I write you this to inform U of some Politocal newse. They are preparing for the election very fast . . . [and] are buying ammunition. The colored folks have got 1600 Army guns. All prepared for busness.

During one campaign in South Carolina, the story was

---

[10] H.R. Rep. 22, Vol. II, Part 3, 42d Cong., 2d Sess., p. 1185.

[11] Verton M. Queener, "A Decade of East Tennessee Republicanism," *The East Tennessee Historical Society's Publications*, Vol. XIV (1942), pp. 59–86.

[12] Herbert, *Why the Solid South?* p. 198.

[13] J. Winsmith to R. K. Scott, September 20, 1870, Robert K. Scott Papers.

[14] J. Crews to Constable —. —. Hubbard, July 8, 1870, quoted in *Report of Joint Investigating Committee on Public Frauds in South Carolina, 1877–1878*, p. 675.

[15] B. F. Eddin to —. —. Thompson, July 31, 1875, quoted in A. T. Morgan, *Yazoo: On the Picket Line of Freedom in the South*, p. 452. (Hereafter cited as *Yazoo*.)

circulated among freedmen that any of them caught voting the Democratic ticket would be shot by the Negro militia.[16]

On election days, troops were very much in evidence around the polls. Their presence was usually tacitly approved by party leaders, and in several instances official sanction was explicitly given. The Governor of Texas, for example, issued a proclamation before the election of 1871 in that state in which he expressly forbade loitering around the polls, jeering at other voters, drinking liquor, or carrying firearms on election day; he instructed "militia on duty at the polls" to enforce the orders.[17] General Joseph A. Cooper, of the Tennessee forces, issued this significantly worded order to his men: "Commanders of companies and detachments of Tennessee State Guards will on the day of election on consultation with their Union friends distribute the men of their commands to the best possible advantage. . . ."[18] As a result, militia forces were almost always to be found around the polls and oftentimes were involved in the frequent election-day disorders and disturbances.[19]

Another area of political action in which the militia participated was the numerous statehouse struggles that took place during the period. The Texas affair offers a typical example. In December, 1873, the faltering Republican cause in Texas was dealt a stunning blow when Judge Richard Coke, the Democratic nominee, defeated Edmund J. Davis, the Radical incumbent, for the governorship.

[16] E. Merton Coulter, *The South during Reconstruction*, p. 355.

[17] Proclamation quoted in Herbert, *Why the Solid South?* pp. 375–76.

[18] Circular 2, issued July 25, 1867, AGO files, state of Tennessee.

[19] Patton, *Reconstruction in Tennessee*, pp. 177–78, 231; Thompson, *Ousting the Carpetbagger from South Carolina*, pp. 72–73; *The Nation*, March 9, 1871.

Davis, in one last desperate attempt at political survival, refused to surrender the office. When Coke arrived in Austin on January 12, 1874, to claim the Statehouse, he found his defeated rival firmly entrenched in the building, guarded by a body of Negro militia.[20] For several days, great excitement prevailed. While Davis awaited a reply to his appeal to Grant for support, the "Travis Rifles," a company of white riflemen, were called up, and open conflict seemed unavoidable. At this point Davis received Grant's telegram refusing to send troops.[21] Seeing the hopelessness of his situation, Davis capitulated, and the Statehouse was taken by Coke and his supporters. Negro militia forces were also present during the Kellogg-McEnery struggle in Louisiana and the Hampton-Chamberlain controversy in South Carolina, and by a curious set of circumstances they fought on both sides during the Brooks-Baxter War in Arkansas.

Still another political function of the militia was the enforcement of gubernatorial declarations of martial law, sometimes levied against counties of dubious political preference. The largest operation of this type occurred in Arkansas. On November 1, 1868, two days before the general election, Governor Clayton informed each state legislator of his intention to declare martial law.[22] A proclamation followed immediately, the effect of which was to throw the state into four months of terrorism.[23] To facilitate execution of the proclamation, the state was divided into four military districts. The District of the South East, comprising seven counties, was placed under command of Colonel S. W. Mallory, and martial law, enforced by three

[20] *Austin* (Texas) *Daily Democratic Statesman*, January 6–9, 1874.
[21] *New York Herald*, January 17, 18, 1874.
[22] J. M. Harrell, *The Brooks and Baxter War*, pp. 66–67.
[23] Clayton, *Aftermath in Arkansas*, p. 63.

NOTICE!

SPECIAL MILITARY TAX!

Office Special Agent, State of Texas,

Groesbeeck, Limestone Co., Texas,

OCTOBER 24th, 1871.

Pursuant to orders received from

Major General H. G. Maloy, commanding State forces in Limestone County, I am ordered to assess and levy a SPECIAL MILITARY TAX OF FORTY THOUSAND DOLLARS, ($40,000 00,) to be paid by the citizens of Limestone County, to defray the expenses of Military Commission and State Troops now on duty in said County.

I therefore levy a Tax of 3 — per cent. on the hundred dollars of all taxable property situated in said County, as per Assessment Rolls of 1871.

All persons owning property in Limestone County are notified to appear at my office, in the city of Groesbeeck, *immediately*, and pay the same. All persons refusing or failing to pay said Tax within three [3] days from above date, ten [10] per cent. will be added, and their property levied upon and sold to satisfy said Tax.

GEO. W. FARROW,

Special Agent State of Texas for Limestone County.

No. _____

Office of Special Agent, State of Texas.

Groesbeeck, *Nov 7* 1871.

Received of *C. G. Andrews*

Eight + 25/100 _____ Dollars,

amount of Military Tax levied upon *him* to defray

expenses of Martial Law in Limestone County.

$ 8 25/100

Wyatt G. Griffin

Special Agent, State of Texas.

Military tax in Texas: Notice (above) and receipt (below)
(Texas State Archives, Austin)

companies of Negro troops, remained in effect in this area until February 6, 1869. The District of the South West, made up of twenty counties, was assigned to R. F. Catterson, former Brigadier General of United States Volunteers. In this district, the proclamation remained effective until January 12, 1869. The District of the North West, thirteen counties in all, was commanded by Colonel J. T. Watson, whose forces consisted of four companies of Negro troops, commanded mostly by white men. The District of the North East, made up of the remaining twenty counties, was under the authority of General D. P. Upham, an unpopular former agent of the Freedmen's Bureau upon whose life one attempt had previously been made. Four Negro companies were included in the forces under his command.[24] Conditions in Arkansas during this period were deplorable:[25]

Many of the best citizens have fled for safety . . . and many others have been arrested. . . . Several men have been shot . . . [and] a large number of horses have been taken. . . . Scarcely a cabin in the county has escaped plunder. This work has been done by the Arkansas militia . . . and has been going on for more than two months with almost incredible shamelessness.

Other states had similar experiences. In Texas, Limestone and Freestone counties were placed under martial law by Governor Davis for a ten-day period in 1871. State troops were called in, and the counties were subsequently assessed $50,000 to defray costs of the operation.[26] The Kirk-Holden War in North Carolina, which lasted from June to No-

[24] For full account of martial law period, see Staples, *Reconstruction in Arkansas*, pp. 295–301; Clayton, *Aftermath in Arkansas*, p. 63 *et passim*.

[25] Thomas Black to Andrew Johnson, January 14, 1869, Andrew Johnson Papers.

[26] Ramsdell, *Reconstruction in Texas*, p. 310.

vember, 1870, is another illustration of the close relationship between martial law and political necessity.

While pursuing these political assignments, the Negro
militia committed certain acts that, although not of a
political nature themselves, did much to aggravate already
strained feelings. When the militia was called into service
anywhere, the Conservative press filled the air with
atrocity stories, many of which have found their way into
literature about the period. It is imperative to point out
that many of these stories were either greatly exaggerated
or entirely untrue. This is not to say, however, that militia
forces were altogether guiltless. The most serious of the
offenses were crimes of violence committed by militiamen
and usually resulted in immediate and fierce retaliation.

Several murders were committed in which state troops
were implicated. One such case occurred in South Carolina
early in 1871. One Matt Stevens, while driving a wagon
loaded with barrels of whisky, was accosted by about forty
of Governor Scott's Negro militia. When Stevens refused
to give up his cargo, an altercation followed during which
Stevens was killed. Reprisals followed immediately.
Thirteen Negro militiamen were arrested and jailed. Five
of these were forcibly taken from confinement; two of
the five were shot to death, and three escaped. While being
moved to Columbia for safekeeping, the remaining eight
prisoners were captured and shot by a large body of armed
and disguised men. It was necessary to send federal troops
to the scene to restore peace.[27]

Less sensational killings involving militiamen took place
in other areas. In December, 1868, in Conway County,
Arkansas, a "disguised party" attacked the home of Alvin

[27] *Charleston Daily News,* January 5, 1871; Reynolds, *Reconstruction in South Carolina,* p. 183; *Harper's Weekly,* April 29, 1871.

and Wash Lewis, two Negroes suspected of living with white prostitutes. Alvin escaped, but the less fortunate Wash was killed. This brought to the scene a Negro militia company under the command of Captain Matthews. Several arrests were made, and one suspect was shot and killed ostensibly while attempting to escape.[28] Similarly, a detachment of militia under Captain W. O. Rickman was involved in the killing of A. P. Brown in Franklin, Tennessee, in May, 1867. Brown had been arrested by Brownlow's militia for suspected bushwhacking and also for having threatened "to clean out" Rickman's company. En route to a place of confinement, Brown made a break for freedom and was shot and killed by a squad of militiamen under Lieutenant Holt.[29] On rare occasions militiamen killed one another in personal disputes.

Several cases of incendiarism were charged against state troops, but the evidence against them was flimsy in the extreme. For instance, a fire broke out in Lewisburg, Arkansas, during the period of martial law in 1868, and the militia forces stationed there at the time were blamed for it.[30] Available evidence suggests that the troops were more concerned with putting out the fire than with starting it. Again, in South Carolina, the so-called "Ned Tennant troubles" in January, 1875, resulted from a fire that broke out on the plantation of M. C. Butler. Tennant, Negro captain of the Edgefield Militia, which had already engaged in one skirmish with the local whites, was charged

[28] *New York Herald*, December 10, 1868; Clayton, *Aftermath in Arkansas*, pp. 153–54.

[29] S. Hunt to W. G. Brownlow, June 3, 1867, AGO files, state of Tennessee. Hunt was the Governor's official representative to investigate and report on this incident.

[30] Clayton, *Aftermath in Arkansas*, p. 155, citing *Daily Arkansas Gazette*, December 20, 1868.

with having started the fire, and a warrant was issued for his arrest. Tennant thereupon mobilized his unit, and when local authorities were unable to make the arrest a posse was formed. The forces collided, and gunfire was exchanged. Tennant was eventually arrested, and his troops turned in their guns at the Edgefield courthouse.[31]

Cases involving militiamen accused of rape or attempted rape occurred infrequently. In late 1868 and early 1869, Arkansas seemed to be plagued with more offenses of this nature than any other Southern state. In December, 1868, four Negro militiamen belonging to a Helena company raped two white women. They were arrested, tried by court-martial, and condemned to be shot. Sentence was carried out by a firing squad composed entirely of Negroes.[32] When General Horace Porter, who had been sent to investigate conditions in Arkansas, reported to his superiors, he cited an instance where a "Negro militiaman committed rape on a white woman" and "was immediately arrested by General Catterson . . . tried, convicted, and promptly executed."[33] Governor Clayton ruefully admitted that there were cases in Arkansas where white women had been violated by Negro militiamen.[34]

Additional cause for bad feelings resulted from militia activities during periods of enforcement of martial law. Arbitrary arrests and lengthy detentions were not unknown,[35] and there were instances where prisoners re-

[31] Francis B. Simkins, *Pitchfork Ben Tillman*, pp. 60–61. See also Reynolds, *Reconstruction in South Carolina*, p. 301.

[32] J. T. Watson to P. Clayton, October 3, 1889, cited in Clayton, *Aftermath in Arkansas*, p. 128. Watson was a colonel in the Arkansas State Militia during the Reconstruction period.

[33] General Horace Porter to U. S. Grant, December 26, 1868, quoted in *New York Tribune*, January 9, 1869.

[34] John Gould Fletcher, *Arkansas*, p. 220.

[35] S. Rep. 1, 24th Cong., 1st Sess., p. 311.

ceived both verbal and physical abuse.[36] Trials by court-martial were held in several states, and in certain extreme cases convicted prisoners were executed.[37] Confiscation of private property by militia forces also occurred, but these losses were in many cases made good by subsequent legislative action.[38] While operating in the field, militia forces also perfected and employed refinements in the art of blackmail. A favorite practice was to extort money from relatives in exchange for the release of a kinsman then in custody of the militia.[39] "Protection papers" were another source of revenue for militiamen. One prisoner paid $150 for immediate release and future immunity, while another, in order to secure the necessary $200 for his freedom, was given a "parole" to go home and raise the cash.[40] "Safeguards," such as the following, were issued by commanders in exchange for specified sums:[41]

Headquarters, North East Arkansas
Augusta, December 29, 1868

A safeguard is hereby granted James B. Currie and family and all property of whatsoever kind belonging to him. All officers and soldiers under this command are therefore commanded to respect this safeguard.

D. P. Upham
Brig. Gen'l, Commanding.

[36] William H. Battle, *The Habeas Corpus Proceedings*, p. 67.

[37] Stokely Morgan was publicly shot after conviction by a military court in Arkansas in 1868. Morgan was tried by military commission for complicity in the brutal murder of a Negro and a deputy sheriff. Clayton, *Aftermath in Arkansas*, pp. 117–18.

[38] Captain Rodney, USA, to Colonel Franks, USA, July 30, 1870, quoted in S. Rep. 1, 42d Cong., 1st Sess., p. lxxvii; Harrell, *The Brooks and Baxter War*, p. 82.

[39] M. Gregory to U. Rose, August 14, 1915, quoted in U. M. Rose, "Clayton's Aftermath of the Civil War in Arkansas," *Publications of the Arkansas Historical Association*, Vol. IV (1917), p. 65.

[40] Harrell, *The Brooks and Baxter War*, p. 82.

[41] *Ibid.*

Less important but equally disturbing were the minor depredations committed by the militia. Brawls were not infrequent. Whenever a militiaman became involved in a street fight, he could generally count on, and usually asked for, the support of his comrades.[42] In February, 1870, a fight between a white resident and a Negro militiaman almost led to a riot in Yorkville, South Carolina. Only through the intervention of a brigadier general of state militia, who rushed by train to the scene, was bloodshed averted.[43] The Laurens, South Carolina, riot of October 20, 1870, in which several Negroes were killed, was precipitated by a fist fight.[44] Additional causes for complaint against the militia resulted from their use of threatening gestures and obscene language.[45] Too, thefts and rumors of thefts were quite common. Militiamen were accused of taking "anything in sight," and one Conservative spokesman complained: "If we have anything . . . they want, they take it . . . curse us for d——d rebels, and say they will pay us back."[46] While they were encamped on the Brownsville, Tennessee, fairgrounds, the freehanded actions of the Tennessee State Guards brought forth this petulant comment: " 'Brownlow's melish' have arrived . . . and their first act was to capture some fifty dollars worth of lumber at the depot on their arrival. Afterwards they directed their attention to robbing of henroosts."[47]

[42] Testimony of James Chesnut, H.R. Rep. 22, Vol. I, Part 3, 42d Cong., 2d Sess., p. 450.

[43] Testimony of Thomas Graham, *ibid.*, p. 711.

[44] *Anderson* (S.C.) *Intelligencer*, October 27, 1870; Reynolds, *Reconstruction in South Carolina*, p. 137; Leland, *A Voice from South Carolina*, p. 52.

[45] —. —. Gamble to J. Cooper, July 14, 1867, AGO files, state of Tennessee. Cooper was in command of the Tennessee State Guard.

[46] *Daily Arkansas Gazette*, December 13, 1868.

[47] *Nashville* (Tenn.) *Union and Dispatch*, February 19, 1867.

Occasional acts that might best be described as social annoyances also caused resentment. For example, the wedding of a prominent local couple in Johnson County, Arkansas, was broken up by a detachment of Negro militia in a still unexplained military diversion. In the subsequent firing, four of the Negroes were wounded.[48] When "Kirk's Lambs," as the North Carolina troops were derisively nicknamed, were stationed at Camp Holden, near Yanceyville, they very nearly provoked a riot by undressing and bathing within full view of the inhabitants of the town.[49] Captain Clingan, of the Tennessee State Guard, aroused the ire of the countryside by having a man ridden out of town on a rail for trying to persuade his Negro soldiers to desert.[50] Governor Holden was roundly denounced by North Carolinians for threatening to use his troops to prevent the arrest of one of his subordinates by the civil authority.[51]

Other annoyances of considerable nuisance value were directly connected with militia drills. According to one report, "They were constantly parading the streets with those guns on their shoulders. You would pass along the road at any time of day and meet these negroes with guns; could hear them firing constantly during the day time and night time."[52] Shots were fired indiscriminately by militiamen going to and returning from musters; using guns furnished them by the state, they frequently visited their spite

[48] Harrell, *The Brooks and Baxter War*, pp. 84–85.

[49] Hamilton, *Reconstruction in North Carolina*, p. 516.

[50] *Nashville* (Tenn.) *Union and Dispatch*, June 1, 1867.

[51] On hearing of the arrest of his auditor, Holden exclaimed: "Supreme Court or no Supreme Court, Chief Justice or no Chief Justice, d——d if my officials shall go to jail. If they do, it shall be over the dead bodies of my militia." (Hamilton, *Reconstruction in North Carolina*, pp. 382–83.)

[52] Testimony of Robert W. Shand, H.R. Rep. 22, Vol. II, Part 3, 42d Cong., 2d Sess., p. 969.

on their white neighbors' property. Livestock and dogs were favorite targets.[53] Numerous crises arose when militia companies marched "company front," thereby forcing whites off the streets. Such a trivial action caused the bloody riot at Hamburg, South Carolina. Moreover, militia captains seem to have felt an irresistible compulsion to deliver inflammatory speeches to their troops. Joe Crews, militia leader in Laurens, South Carolina, was quoted as telling his men that they must never unite with the whites in any movement and that if they wanted provisions and could not afford them they should go into the fields and take what they wanted. If whites did not settle with them the way they thought was right, then they should burn them out of house and home. He added that matches were cheap.[54] Such speeches, received with great enthusiasm by the assembled troops, served only to enrage the already suspicious whites.

Perhaps the greatest nuisance of all was the incessant noise of the militia drills. A favorite trick of men returning from muster was to scrape a bayonet rapidly along a picket fence, arousing all light sleepers within a considerable radius.[55] Every drill squad somehow managed to obtain a drum, and the evening calm was shattered by the steady cadence of drum beats. Many fights resulted from attempts of whites to silence these nocturnal poundings.[56] Drummer boys were often singled out for individual attention at the none-too-tender hands of antimilitia groups.[57]

[53] Testimony of James Chesnut, *ibid.,* p. 467.
[54] *Columbia* (S.C.) *Daily Phoenix,* September 7, 1870.
[55] James Brewster, *Sketches of Southern Mystery, Treason, and Murder,* p. 165. (Hereafter cited as *Sketches.*)
[56] A good example is the riot at New Hope Church, Mississippi, in September, 1875. (*Harper's Weekly,* September 11, 1875.)
[57] Testimony of Wesley Alexander, *Report of Evidence Taken be-*

Certain more favored militia units had, besides drummers, full-scale military bands that enthusiastically contributed to the din. Band members sometimes added other duties to their roles as musicians, as is strongly suggested by the following request from a bandleader to the Radical governor of his state: "I would like to borrow about 24 guns for the use of our brass band...."[58]

Before we consider specific case histories of militia activities, it should be re-emphasized that the purpose of this chapter is not to compile a catalogue of sins with which to condemn the militia but to furnish sufficient factual data in order to arrive at something like a true picture of the movement. As the reader will see, militia activities were not in themselves the real reason for the eventual destruction of the forces, but they kept alive the intense racial feeling that made destruction inevitable.

From the foregoing survey, certain generalizations can be made. First, although originally organized as a protective device, militia forces were inevitably converted into aggressive political instruments. Second, participation in politics as well as the resulting depredations, disturbances, and minor social annoyances were the immediate causes for the expressed hostility of the Conservatives. Finally, crimes of violence committed by militiamen were so infrequent that they can be dismissed as the inevitable concomitant of protracted military activity. In viewing the over-all militia operations in the South during Reconstruction, one's reaction is not so much horror at an excessive number of unlawful acts committed as surprise that there were no more.

---

fore the *Military Committee, 35th General Assembly, State of Tennessee, 1868,* p. 26.

[58] H. Smith to A. Ames, August 30, 1875, quoted in S. Rep. 527, 44th Cong., 1st Sess., p. 25.

IV. Minstrels and Brindle-Tails

AMONG THE GRIM IRONIES of Reconstruction, none was more prophetic than the fact that Arkansas, after the inauguration of Governor Clayton in July, 1868, was welcomed back to the sisterhood of states with a military salute of fifteen guns. This was a most fitting celebration, since that turbulent state would continue to hear sporadic firing for another six years. A not inconsiderable amount of this gunfire was directly connected with the Negro militia, for in no other Southern state were these forces used as often or as actively as in Arkansas.

The first wave of militia activity resulted from the Governor's declaration of martial law, which lasted from November, 1868, to February, 1869, as related in Chapter III. This remedy failed to cure any fundamental political sickness in that most afflicted state, and the social unrest, mobilization of Negro troops, and resulting violence were mere harbingers of things to come. In the spring of 1874, political difficulties were to throw the state into a full-fledged civil war, and Negro farmers were once more to leave their fields to enroll in the military forces of the state. But this time the circumstances would be considerably different. Both parties in the struggle would be made up of Arkansas Republicans, and, as is so often the case when good friends fall out, the fight would be a fierce one.

The background for the so-called "Brooks-Baxter War" of April, 1874, is entwined in the elusive political history of the preceding years. Powell Clayton, who had come to Arkansas with the Union Army and had decided to remain, was elected governor in 1868 and held that office until March, 1871, when he entered the United States Senate. During his exceedingly active administration, the

Republican party in Arkansas was faced with the serious problem of internal division. Clayton, while essentially a courageous man, was wanting in the tact and foresight that are so necessary in order to unite disparate segments into a homogeneous party.[1] For two years, he successfully prevented a schism, but seeds of discord were firmly planted in the political soil of Arkansas, and visible signs of dissension had appeared as early as 1870. When Clayton resigned the governorship in order to take a Senate seat, his continued control of the state was practically assured through a maneuver that brought O. A. Hadley, for many years a Clayton satellite, into the executive mansion. Hadley was even less adept than his predecessor in political diplomacy, and during his brief administration the party split wide open. This splintering resulted from two circumstances. The increasingly bitter political enmities on the local scene made it impossible for contending factions to operate within the framework of one party. Too, Arkansas was only a microcosm of the national political scene, where the Republican party was being ripped by the Liberal Republican revolt. The bolters in Arkansas rallied to the standard of Joseph Brooks, an erstwhile evangelist from Iowa who had first come to Arkansas as chaplain to a Negro regiment of United States troops.[2] The Regular Republicans remained under Clayton's control.

The election of 1872 brought the intraparty battle into the open, and each group nominated a complete ticket. The Liberal faction, with Brooks as its candidate, began an all-

[1] Staples, *Reconstruction in Arkansas*, pp. 276–78.

[2] Fletcher, *Arkansas*, p. 206. Clayton, in reference to Brooks, once said, "With the exception of myself, he perhaps was . . . the most unpopular man in the whole state." (Clayton, *Aftermath in Arkansas*, p. 347.)

out war on the Clayton group. The Regular Republicans chose Elisha Baxter, a quiet, hard-working former circuit judge as their nominee. Baxter's two most prominent qualifications seem to have been his indictment for treason by the Confederacy and his freedom from any participation in the shady financial deals of the Clayton era. The Baxter ticket endorsed the Grant administration, while the Brooks group pledged itself to support Horace Greeley and Gratz Brown.[3] The Democrats, in order to play their advantage to the hilt, made no nominations themselves but informally agreed to support Brooks, largely because he was anti-Clayton.

A very lively campaign ensued, and the two wings of the shattered Republican party received nicknames destined to become part of the political vocabulary of Arkansas. The Clayton supporters, or Regulars, were dubbed "minstrels." Although the actual reason for the name is unknown, one authority suggests that it was derived from the fact that the Regulars sang "more sweetly to Clayton's ears." The Brooks followers became known as "Brindle-Tails" as a result of a Brooks follower's comparison of his leader to a brindle-tail bull that "bellowed so loud that it scared all the other cattle half to death."[4] Republican versus Republican produced a campaign as lively and interesting as any two-party contest before or since. Negro Republicans in one group used many of the generally recognized Conservatives clichés to describe the shortcomings of Negroes on the other side. Prominent carpetbaggers outstripped one another in denouncing carpetbaggery,[5] and

---

[3] *American Annual Cyclopaedia, 1874*, p. 37.

[4] Fletcher, *Arkansas*, p. 230.

[5] One group of Negro soldiers voiced the sentiment that "no damned carpet-bagger would be allowed to stay in the country." Their leader,

Brooks set the tone of the campaign by declaring that if he was elected he would fill the county jail "so full of Clayton's followers that their arms and legs would stick out of the windows."[6]

The election of November 5 was accompanied by many irregularities. Members of the state militia, now legally under Hadley's control but actually still at the disposal of Clayton, were placed around the polls. When the results were officially announced in the Legislature, Baxter was declared the victor and duly installed.[7] Brooks attempted to obtain an injunction in the United States courts to prevent Baxter's accession, but the case was thrown out.[8] A subsequent appeal to the Legislature was also rejected. Finally, in desperation, Brooks filed suit against Baxter in the Pulaski County Court, but it was by this time generally assumed that nothing would come of the action. Subsequent events were to prove this one of the great miscalculations in Arkansas politics of that decade.

Fifteen months later, on April 15, 1874, the Pulaski court rendered a surprise decision, apparently based more on politics than on law, favoring Brooks.[9] Armed with a court order and surrounded by loyal supporters, among whom was General Catterson, of earlier martial-law fame, Brooks invaded the Statehouse and ordered Baxter out.[10] When he refused to leave, Baxter was forcibly ejected from the office by two of Catterson's men. As he was led from the

John J. Williams, was the most prominent local carpetbagger. (Testimony of John Ellis, H.R. Rep. 2, 43d Cong., 2d Sess., p. 345.)

[6] Fletcher, *Arkansas*, p. 231.

[7] *Ibid.*

[8] *American Annual Cyclopaedia, 1874*, p. 38.

[9] *Ibid.*

[10] *Van Buren* (Ark.) *Free Press*, April 21, 1874; Fletcher, *Arkansas*, p. 234, *American Annual Cyclopaedia, 1874*, p. 38.

room, he turned to his rivals and slowly, deliberately, and prophetically announced: "You will hear from me again soon."[11]

The next five days were marked by feverish activity as both sides took steps to solidify their positions. Brooks settled down in the Statehouse with approximately 300 armed men, mostly Negroes, on guard.[12] The Baxter forces set up headquarters in the Anthony House, a favorite political gathering place in Little Rock, appropriately situated within easy gunshot of the Statehouse.[13] Arkansas now had two governors, both of whom were frantically sending claims of legitimacy to President Grant. Brooks sent a telegram to Grant claiming to be the legal governor of Arkansas and requested that the state arms in storage at the federal arsenal be delivered to him.[14] Baxter simultaneously reported the details of his ouster to the President, and although he expressed hope that the dispute would be settled "without bloodshed," he stated his firm intention "to take measures immediately to resume possession of the state property" and to maintain his authority as rightful governor.[15] The President, acting through his Attorney General, George H. Williams, answered both claimants on the following day. Perhaps previous reactions to his Southern policy had made him cautious, for, without recognizing the authority of either, he refused to allow Brooks to secure guns from the arsenal[16] or to send troops to support Baxter.[17]

[11] Fletcher, *Arkansas*, p. 235.

[12] *Ibid.*, p. 236.

[13] *American Annual Cyclopaedia, 1874*, p. 38.

[14] Joseph Brooks to Ulysses S. Grant, April 15, 1874, quoted in *ibid.*, p. 39.

[15] Elisha Baxter to Ulysses S. Grant, April 15, 1874, quoted in *ibid.*

[16] Ulysses S. Grant to Joseph Brooks, April 16, 1874, quoted in *ibid.*

[17] Ulysses S. Grant to Elisha Baxter, April 16, 1874, quoted in *ibid.*

Baxter thereupon declared martial law in Pulaski County, in which the state capital, Little Rock, was situated.[18] He reorganized the militia forces, placing them under command of General Robert C. Newton, a former Confederate officer.[19] At the same time, Brooks issued an order revoking all Baxter's militia appointments, announced his own selections, and placed supreme command in the hands of James F. Fagan, also a former Confederate.[20] All in all, the scene was ludicrously reminiscent of that unseemly period in medieval church history when rival popes exchanged anathema and excommunicated one another. While these scenes were being enacted, Captain T. E. Rose, commanding the federal troops stationed in Little Rock and acting on orders from Washington, issued warnings to both sides to avoid conflict.[21]

Meanwhile, both sides continued preparations for war. Arms were zealously sought by Brooks and Baxter supporters. Attempts to borrow guns from the Federal arsenal met with flat refusal from Captain Rose. Brooks forces broke into the state arsenal and took a hundred rifles and two cannons, which were strategically placed around the Statehouse.[22] A personal friend of Brooks's named McDiarmid was sent to St. Louis to procure arms on the basis of a $50,000 appropriation Brooks claimed to have obtained. His efforts were amply rewarded: 2,000 Springfield rifles, 13,000 rounds of ammunition, and several cases of revolvers were shipped into Little Rock for Brooks partisans. The occupants of the Statehouse were also supplied with several

[18] *Van Buren* (Ark.) *Free Press,* April 21, 1867.
[19] Fletcher, *Arkansas,* p. 239.
[20] Harrell, *The Brooks and Baxter War,* p. 207.
[21] *American Annual Cyclopaedia, 1874,* p. 41.
[22] Harrell, *The Brooks and Baxter War,* p. 214.

carloads of provisions in preparation for an extended siege.[23] Baxter adherents were not idle either. The stocks of three local gun merchants were seized and issued to recruits as they arrived.[24] The deposed Governor sent William E. Woodruff as his personal envoy to Texas on a gun-raising expedition,[25] while on the local scene some of the more fervent Baxterites unearthed a 64-pound siege gun that had lain encrusted in riverbank mud for the nine long years since the end of the war. Unofficially christened "Lady Baxter," it was unspiked and refurbished and then hauled to the Anthony House lawn, where, aimed forbiddingly in the general direction of the enemy, it enjoyed one last moment of glory before being honorably retired, with a suitably inscribed plaque, to a place of distinction on the Statehouse grounds to receive homage from future generations of sightseers.

Reinforcements, primarily for Baxter, poured into Little Rock from all directions, coming by horseback, wagon, train, and boat. Upon arrival, they were sworn into the Arkansas State Guard, armed, and assigned a billet. The most colorful leader to emerge on either side was H. King White, twenty-eight-year-old veteran of Morgan's Raiders, a swashbuckler to the core.[26] At the outset of the trouble, he had telegraphed Baxter promising to "furnish 1,000 men, if necessary, to reinstate you."[27] He kept his promise. On Saturday, April 18, the steamer *Mary Boyd* arrived in Little Rock bearing White and his army of 300 "strawhatted,

[23] Benjamin S. Johnson, "The Brooks-Baxter War," *Publications of the Arkansas Historical Association*, Vol. II (1908), pp. 145–46.

[24] Fletcher, *Arkansas*, p. 241.

[25] *Ibid.*, p. 252.

[26] Harrell, *The Brooks and Baxter War*, p. 230.

[27] King White to Elisha Baxter, April 16, 1874, quoted in *ibid.*, p. 216.

coatless, and largely unarmed mob of Negro field hands."[28] Greeted by an imposing array of local dignitaries in a ceremony complete with brass band and martial tunes, the Negroes paraded from the landing to the Anthony House headquarters, singing what was to become known as the "Baxter Song:"[29]

> Do you see that boat come around the bend?
> Goodbye, my lover, goodbye;
> It's loaded down with Baxter men.
> Goodbye, my lover, goodbye!

Another boatload of Baxter troops arrived aboard the *Kitty Hegler*. The owner, J. D. Hegler, of Cincinnati, hoping to make a quick profit as a troop-carrier, took on a load of Negro soldiers at Pine Bluff. Hegler's hopes were blighted by his foraging passengers, who, before reaching Little Rock, had succeeded in looting his cargo "to the amount of a thousand dollars" in liquor, canned fruit, and candy.[30]

Behind all these preparations for war, strange things were happening in the political field. In a dazzling display of political footwork, earlier alignments were exactly reversed, and most of the Regular Republicans, following the lead of the unpredictable Clayton, swung over to the support of Brooks.[31] This came about as a result of Clayton's discovery that Baxter, as governor, intended to make his own decisions.[32] After a quarrel over calling up the militia, during which Baxter flatly refused to comply with

[28] Fletcher, *Arkansas*, p. 241.

[29] *Ibid.*

[30] Testimony of J. D. Hegler, H.R. Rep. 2, 43d Cong., 2d Sess., p. 370.

[31] Clayton, *Aftermath in Arkansas*, p. 348.

[32] Baxter later said, "I had to choose between being their tool or their enemy." (Printed statement of Elisha Baxter, April 28, 1874, in the possession of the author.)

The Brooks-Baxter War in Arkansas (Harper's Weekly, *1874*)

Clayton's demands, the latter joined forces with Brooks, creating an alliance that caused one politician of the day to recall with some humor the campaign of 1872, in which "Mr. Brooks was painted blacker than midnight darkness by the very men who today are trying to make him governor of Arkansas."[33] Original Brooksites, more from anti-Clayton feeling than anything else—but also prompted by the knowledge that during his short term Baxter had proved a capable and honest administrator—moved into the ever widening circle around the Anthony House. This amazing political about-face was accompanied by considerable name-calling and bad feeling, and the mounting number of reinforcements arriving daily turned Little Rock into an armed camp.[34]

As so frequently occurs when belligerents are fully armed, they stumbled into a fight accidentally. Late in the afternoon of April 21, King White held a dress parade to show off his army, which had by then grown to nearly 2,000 men. Using the much-sought-after military band, he marched his troops through the streets of Little Rock for almost an hour before drawing them up in formation before the Anthony House. The militiamen clamored for Baxter, who presently appeared on the hotel balcony to address them.[35] He recounted the events that had led up to the present situation and reiterated his intention of retaking the office but refused to give any definite orders, saying:[36]

Officers and commanders cannot give, in advance to the troops or to the country, a detailed account of their proposed opera-

[33] Speech of W. W. Wilshire delivered in Arkansas House of Representatives, May 28, 1874. (Copy in the possession of the author.)
[34] *New York Herald*, April 19, 1874; *The Independent*, May 7, 1874.
[35] *Daily Arkansas Gazette*, April 22, 1874.
[36] Harrell, *The Brooks and Baxter War*, p. 226.

tions. They are necessarily military secrets; they are matters which necessarily must be kept quiet; and you will not expect of me on an occasion as public as this to detail my plan of operation.

At this juncture, the impetuous White interrupted and asked pointedly whether or not Baxter planned to have them take the Statehouse.[37] Baxter replied by cautioning the men to restrain themselves and had begun to leave the balcony when King White, all the while protesting that he had not, of course, come to make a speech, made a very fiery one indeed:[38]

I have brought with me here a number of colored men. It has been said, sir, that these colored men will prove treacherous to you. I now ask these colored men, in your presence, and in the presence of this assemblage, whether we shall stand firm to Elisha Baxter?

Warming to his task, White continued:

Furnish us simply with the means—give us the authority—pronounce the order, and I will guarantee to you, sir, that in twenty five minutes from the time the order is written, Joseph Brooks will either be in hell or the archives. . . .

Baxter thanked White, expressed his own great confidence in the Negro soldiers, and withdrew with the admonition to "be patient, conduct yourselves orderly, and have no fear for the consequences."

The Negro band had just struck up a lively tune when the incident occurred that precipitated the general outbreak. White gave the order for his troops to march. Captain Rose, who had been watching the scene from horseback nearby, fearing that White planned to move against

[37] Fletcher, *Arkansas*, p. 247.
[38] Harrell, *The Brooks and Baxter War*, pp. 226, 227.

the Brooks forces, suddenly spurred his horse toward White, accidentally knocking down two of the musicians. When Rose reached White, angry words were exchanged. White warned Rose that he would not be permitted to ride over the Negro soldiers, even if he was an officer of the United States. Rose hotly ordered White to keep his place and to restrain his men, to which White answered: "You are an officer and should be a gentleman. Whether you are or not, I am; I'll not permit you to ride over my men nor over me, sir." What happened next is a matter of dispute. One account says Rose drew his pistol and fired at White. Another claims that one of the Negroes fired at Rose. At any rate, a shot rang out, which was the signal for an outbreak of indiscriminate firing that lasted for about five minutes.

When the shooting died down after this first battle of the Brooks-Baxter War, the casualty list was hardly a tribute to the marksmanship of either side. An elderly citizen of Little Rock, D. Y. Shall, who had been enjoying the scene from a window in the Anthony House, was shot through the head and died within an hour. One of Brooks's "colonels" was shot through both legs, and several soldiers on both sides were wounded. Other casualties included a chambermaid who unwisely jumped from an upstairs window of the Anthony House in her excitement, and one Reverend Gillem, a Negro divine, who was badly cut when he spectacularly leaped through the glass door of a store to make way for the combatants. By nightfall, quiet had been restored.[39]

Three immediate repercussions were felt from this initial engagement. The first was the issuance of a general

[39] Fletcher, *Arkansas*, p. 248; Harrell, *The Brooks and Baxter War*, pp. 228–29.

order closing "all establishments selling intoxicants" in Little Rock until further notice, an act wisely calculated to lower the martial spirit on both sides.[40] The second was a proclamation by Baxter calling the Legislature into extraordinary session to convene May 11.[41] The third was a telegram from President Grant to Baxter expressing the unlikely hope "that the military forces will now be disbanded."[42] The forces were not disbanded, and Little Rock remained in an unsettled and agitated state. Protests began to be voiced by taxpayers in general and by merchants in particular.[43] One such report reached the desk of President Grant:[44]

The country is now full of marauding parties recruiting soldiers, and unless soon checked and sent home will degenerate into a band of robbers. To sustain their lawless, idle vagabondism, they offer their dupes $22 a month and board to enlist on their side. Where, sir, is the money to come from to pay and support these betrayed poor negroes who leave their crops and families? . . .

The war languished in Little Rock after the first explosion, largely because King White and his troops had been evacuated to Pine Bluff. But if quiet reigned in the capital city, such was not the case in the provinces. The pugnacious White, still eager for a fight, soon found an excuse for one. A Brooks supporter named Murphy recruited a company of some 200 Negroes at New Gascony, approximately 15 miles from Pine Bluff. White, chafing

[40] General Order 16, April 22, 1875, Adjutant-General's Office files, State of Arkansas. (Hereafter cited as AGO files, state of Arkansas.)

[41] *American Annual Cyclopaedia, 1874*, p. 43.

[42] Ulysses S. Grant to Elisha Baxter, April 22, 1874, cited in Harrell, *The Brooks and Baxter War*, p. 231.

[43] Johnson, "The Brooks-Baxter War," pp. 155–56.

[44] C. Taylor to Ulysses S. Grant, April 27, 1874, quoted in S. Exec. Doc. 51, 43d Cong., 1st Sess., p. 5.

under forced inactivity, decided to make a move. On the morning of April 30, he loaded 200 of his Negro militiamen aboard the steamer *Hallie* and sailed for New Gascony. Murphy's men were gathered at Cornerstone Church preparing for a parade.[45] White arrived without being discovered, landed his forces, mounted them on horses pressed into service for the occasion, and charged the surprised Murphy forces. The latter retreated behind a nearby fence and opened fire, but the charge had done its work. The Murphy troops were routed, and Murphy himself was shot in the head, taken prisoner, and lodged in the jail at Pine Bluff. Nine of Murphy's troopers were killed and twenty-odd wounded, while White suffered only four casualties in this most furious single encounter of the war.[46]

The last significant engagement took place on May 7 and was, oddly enough, something of an amphibious operation. The Baxter forces learned that a shipment of arms for the enemy was on its way downriver by flatboat. General Newton detailed forty men to sail aboard the *Hallie* to intercept the guns. Their clandestine departure at three in the morning did not, however, escape the watchful eyes of the Brooksites. Upon receipt of this news, General Fagan sent some of his men by train ahead of the *Hallie* and ordered them to prepare an ambush near Palarm Creek. One officer walked back upriver in an attempt to persuade the *Hallie* to turn back. His shouts were ignored, however, and as the riverboat came abreast of the camouflaged Brooksites, a volley was fired. Several men aboard the *Hallie* were killed, and every man but one was wounded. The ship was damaged in the exchange and drifted helplessly to the op-

[45] Fletcher, *Arkansas*, pp. 238–51.
[46] *Harper's Weekly*, May 16, 1874; Harrell, *The Brooks and Baxter War*, p. 238.

posite side of the river, where those who were able escaped. The ill-starred *Hallie* was taken back to Little Rock, a prize of the Brooks forces, to be scuttled shortly thereafter under cover of darkness by persons unknown. As a result of this engagement the Baxter men who had participated, or what was left of them, were officially designated the "Hallie Rifles."[47]

Meanwhile, pressure from Washington was increasing. On May 9, Attorney General Williams informed both claimants that settlement of the question by the gathering legislators would be considered binding. He beseeched both men to disband their forces.[48] Baxter's refusal caused the President to send a personal request to each side for disbandment, and this time Brooks refused.[49] With matters practically at a standstill, the extraordinary session of the Legislature convened and promptly sent a resolution to Grant that led to the issuance, on May 15, of a Presidential proclamation recognizing Baxter as the legal governor of Arkansas and ordering the Brooks forces "to disperse and return peaceably to their respective abodes within ten days. . . ."[50] Generals Newton and Fagan conferred and agreed on terms of disbandment, which provided for the surrender of state arms, immunity from assault to the losers, and state-subsidized transportation back to their homes.[51]

[47] Fletcher, *Arkansas*, pp. 256–57. A portrait of the *Hallie* encounter can be seen in the museum of the Arkansas Historical Commission in Little Rock.

[48] Dispatch from Attorney-General G. H. Williams to both "governors," May 9, 1874, quoted in *American Annual Cyclopaedia, 1874*, p. 44.

[49] *Ibid.*, p. 45.

[50] Proclamation dated May 15, 1874, quoted in Harrell, *The Brooks and Baxter War*, p. 256.

[51] General Order 10, May 16, 1874, AGO files, state of Arkansas.

The war was over. But before returning to the mundane pursuits of everyday life, King White held one last grand review of the Baxter forces, and his faithful Negro troops left Little Rock as they had entered it, singing. When the last chorus of "We'll Hang Joe Brooks to a Sour Apple Tree" had died down[52] and the last militiaman had returned to his fields, the results of the war seemed pathetic indeed. Beyond doubt, the state Republican party had suffered a blow from which it has not yet recovered, for within a few short months the Democrats were to return to power under the leadership of A. H. Garland. Only Joe Brooks really salvaged anything: President Grant appointed him postmaster of Little Rock.[53] Even more ironic is the fact that the Negroes had been called to arms to fight in behalf of two white claimants for the governorship, as a consequence of which the Negro was eliminated as a political factor in Arkansas.

[52] Fletcher, *Arkansas*, p. 263.
[53] *The Nation*, April 1, 1875.

V. Another Battle of New Orleans

THE BLOODIEST SINGLE ENCOUNTER of the entire Reconstruction period in which Negro militia forces were engaged was fought in New Orleans on September 14, 1874. Late in the afternoon of that day, two armed groups clashed in a full-scale pitched battle as the White Leaguers fought against a combined force of Negro militia and metropolitan police. In this short but fierce struggle over a hundred men were wounded and twenty-odd corpses littered the streets of the city.

Had nothing else occurred during the period, this incident alone would make it worth while to trace the story of the Negro militia in Louisiana. However, as one painfully unravels this tale from the confusing maze of local politics, other pertinent facts emerge. Nowhere else in the South were federal troops so freely employed to do or undo the work of the militia. Nowhere else were the militia forces so exclusively the governor's private army, consistently used either in the furtherance of his own political career or in opposition to another's. And nowhere else could one witness the incongruous spectacle of one of the half-dozen most famous of all Confederate generals riding at the head of a column of Negro militiamen in one last exercise of military command.

The roots of the militia movement in Louisiana go back to the period just after the close of the war. In February, 1866, a rising young politician named Henry Clay Warmoth, a former Union Army officer turned New Orleans lawyer, wrote this account of the attitude of many Louisiana residents: "They openly declare that when the military is removed they will make it too hot here for Union men; and only a few days ago I heard a young man on the streets say that 'hereafter a northern man might just as well be in hell as try to live here.' "[1] When Warmoth was inaugurated as governor two years later, local sentiment had apparently not abated. The law passed by Congress in March, 1867, prohibiting the organization of militia forces in the Southern states was strictly observed by Warmoth even though he complained that "it strips me of all power."[2] The resulting weakness of his administration was fully appreciated by his opponents, for violence continued apace. In September, 1868, the Opelousas riot erupted, and from then until the general election on November 4 the state underwent a reign of terror. During all these disorders, Warmoth remained practically helpless; time and again he was forced to appeal for aid to the federal commander stationed in New Orleans.[3]

Upon repeal of the militia prohibition in 1869,[4] Warmoth took immediate steps to remedy his deplorable lack of armed forces. As a result of his insistent urging, the Legislature passed a militia bill in early April, 1870, authorizing the organization of a militia and appropriating $100,000 to carry the law into effect.[5] The organization and subsequent use of this militia must be considered as a part of the larger story of internal political struggle in Louisiana, and in order to reconstruct the story in its en-

[1] Henry C. Warmoth, *Letter of H. C. Warmoth, Claimant of a Seat in the House of Representatives as a Delegate from the Territory of Louisiana*, p. 33.

[2] H. C. Warmoth, *War, Politics, and Reconstruction: Stormy Days in Louisiana*, p. 76. (Hereafter cited as *War, Politics, and Reconstruction*.)

[3] On October 25, 1868, for example, Warmoth issued the following appeal to General Lovell Rousseau: "I am compelled to appeal to you to take charge of the peace in these parishes and to use your forces to that end." (*Ibid.*)

[4] *Congressional Globe*, 40th Cong., 3d Sess., p. 325.

[5] Lonn, *Reconstruction in Louisiana*, p. 65.

tirety, a survey of the local political scene becomes imperative.

As in several other Southern states, the Radical party that emerged triumphant in Louisiana as a result of the Reconstruction acts enjoyed a relatively short period of unity and was then rent by internal strife. The split among Louisiana Republicans began as early as 1870, when the anti-Warmoth group opposed the Governor in his successful maneuver to remove the restriction making him ineligible for re-election. Open rupture between the two wings of the party took place during the state convention of August, 1871. In the resulting coalitions, Governor Warmoth was supported by P. B. S. Pinchback, a Negro politician who exercised considerable influence over members of his race, while the opposition formed what became known in local circles as the "Custom-House" faction. The latter was built around the combined forces of United States Marshal S. B. Packard; George W. Carter, speaker of the House of Representatives; and J. F. Casey, brother-in-law of President Grant and collector of customs for the port of New Orleans. Actually, two conventions were held simultaneously; the Warmoth group met in Turner's Hall, and the Packard faction held closed sessions in the Custom House.[6]

The first test of strength between the two forces took place in November, 1871. On the twenty-second of that month, Lieutenant Governor Oscar Dunn died, and both factions attempted to install their men in the office.[7] Warmoth won by arranging for the election of Pinchback as president of the Senate, thereby automatically placing him

6 *Ibid.*, pp. 10, 102.
7 Alcée Fortier, *A History of Louisiana*, Vol. IV, p. 117. Subsequent citations to this work refer to Vol. IV.

next in line for the governorship. Whether or not the charges of bribery levied against Warmoth were true, there can be no doubt that his victory only widened the party breach.

When the Legislature reconvened in January, 1872, the bad feeling led to the outbreak of the Carter-Warmoth feud, during which the Louisiana Militia were organized and used for the first time. The feud was essentially a struggle to control the Legislature. On January 4, Speaker Carter was expelled from his position amid great confusion and excitement, and a Warmoth man was installed in his place.[8] The ousted Carter gathered his followers, moved into a room over the Gem Saloon on Royal Street, and set up another legislative body.[9]

The existence of this rival body spurred Warmoth into action, and he decided to call up the militia. In looking around earlier for a satisfactory leader, his eye had fallen upon James A. Longstreet, Lee's former corps commander who in 1866 had settled down in New Orleans to the routine life of a cotton-broker.[10] Longstreet's willingness to be reconstructed cost him both social and business standing in New Orleans, but President Grant, an old Army friend (in whose wedding, incidentally, Longstreet had been best man), appointed him surveyor of customs in New Orleans in March, 1869.[11] Warmoth followed suit by appointing him adjutant general of the state militia on May 13, 1870, with an annual salary of $3,000.[12] When the situation grew threatening in 1872, Longstreet was

[8] Lonn, *Reconstruction in Louisiana*, p. 119.

[9] Fortier, *A History of Louisiana*, p. 118.

[10] H. J. Eckenrode and B. Conrad, *James Longstreet: Lee's War Horse*, pp. 372–75. (Hereafter cited as *James Longstreet*.)

[11] Hesseltine, *U. S. Grant, Politician*, p. 153.

[12] D. B. Sanger and T. R. Hay, *James Longstreet*, p. 349.

placed in a position of active command upon receipt of the following letter, dated January 6: [13]

General: I have the honor to hand you herewith a commission constituting you Major General of Louisiana State Militia, and by order of his excellency the governor, to state that you are thereunder assigned to the immediate command and supervision of the entire militia, police, and all civil forces of the State of Louisiana and within the city of New Orleans.

O. D. Bragdon

Private Secy.

As a result of this communication, Longstreet found himself in command of a strange force. Warmoth had found it "judicious" to arm and organize some 2,500 whites, "notwithstanding the fact they were soldiers in the Confederate Army," and another 2,500 Negroes.[14] The metropolitan police, under Superintendent A. S. Badger, were incorporated into the militia and were armed with Winchester rifles, breech-loading guns, and a 6-pound howitzer.[15]

By this time, a triangular situation existed in New Orleans. Warmoth and his legislature were in the Statehouse, protected by the militia and police; Carter and his legislature were in the Gem Saloon building, surrounded by a large number of deputized citizens; and a detachment of United States troops under General W. H. Emory stood by for any possible emergency.

On January 10, the Warmoth faction took forcible possession of the Gem building without any real opposition.

[13] H.R. Misc. Doc. 211, 42d Cong., 2d Sess., p. 811; Sanger and Hay, *James Longstreet*, p. 356.

[14] H.R. Misc. Doc. 211, 42d Cong., 2d Sess., p. 295.

[15] Testimony of A. S. Badger, *ibid.*, p. 103.

The dispossessed Carterites reassembled in the Cosmopolitan Club[16] and from this new headquarters mounted a premature counterattack that ended in a blustering and bloodless failure to take the Statehouse. Failing in his attempt to gain the support of federal troops, Carter sensed that he must either make a decisive move or surrender. On Saturday, January 20, therefore, thousands of circulars were distributed calling for a mass meeting on Monday and urging Negroes in particular to take arms against "Warmoth and his thieving crew."[17] On Sunday night, the Algiers armory was broken into by Carter followers, and the arms in storage there were distributed among the men.[18] The next day, several thousand men assembled in answer to Carter's appeal and were preparing to march on the Statehouse when word arrived that President Grant had telegraphed General Emory to use his troops if necessary to prevent violence.[19] The President's action made a Warmoth victory certain, and the Carterites returned to the Legislature on the Governor's terms. The state militia, on its first assignment, had been used primarily for guard duty and had not been called upon to do any actual fighting. Relative quiet returned to Louisiana, and within a few weeks General Longstreet was able to resign his command, giving as his reason the somewhat significant desire to remain "untrammeled in the approaching political canvass."[20]

[16] Fortier, *A History of Louisiana*, p. 118.
[17] Circular reprinted in H.R. Misc. Doc. 211, 42d Cong., 2d Sess., pp. 318–19.
[18] Lonn, *Reconstruction in Louisiana*, p. 132.
[19] *American Annual Cyclopaedia, 1872*, p. 472.
[20] J. A. Longstreet to H. C. Warmoth, April 19, 1872, Henry Clay Warmoth Papers.

The next period of militia activity resulted from the confusing election of 1872. The split in the party was widened when one side joined forces with the Liberal Republican movement, which was then under way on the national scene. Both factions decided to enter a ticket. Warmoth broke with Grant and threw his support to the Liberal Republican movement while the Custom House group, with S. B. Packard now in control, continued behind the Grant administration. These two factions were not the only ones, however, for at one time as many as five different slates were offered to the Louisiana voter. Out of this situation several political shifts developed. Warmoth, strangely enough, joined with the Democrats, who for years had been implacable in their opposition to him, to support a fusion ticket headed by John McEnery and D. B. Penn. Pinchback, lieutenant-governor by the grace of Warmoth, deserted his benefactor and joined the Custom House group in support of another fusion ticket, led by William Pitt Kellogg and C. C. Antoine.[21]

The election was held on November 4, and hardly had the last ballot been cast when each side began charging fraud. To complicate the situation further, two returning boards emerged, each supporting the legitimacy of a different candidate. This distressing condition continued until the Legislature convened. A few days before that occasion, however, the Packard forces obtained a court order from Judge E. H. Durrell authorizing them to take over Mechanics Institute, the site of the scheduled legislative session.[22] Packard accomplished this with the aid of federal troops. When the Legislature eventually met, its first

21 Lonn, *Reconstruction in Louisiana*, p. 161.
22 *Ibid.*, p. 194.

acts were to impeach Warmoth, install Pinchback as governor, and proclaim Kellogg and Antoine the victors in the recent election.

In the meantime, Warmoth and his supporters organized their forces in Lyceum Hall, and once again Louisiana had two legislatures. On January 13, the climax of the comedy was reached when two governors were added to the growing list of officeholders: Kellogg was inaugurated in Mechanics Institute while McEnery was taking the same oath in Lafayette Square.

The comedy was not without its grim side. Pinchback called up the militia, alerted the police, and armed both forces. Longstreet, originally hired by Warmoth, was persuaded to return again to his post of command in the militia, now to be used against Warmoth.[23] McEnery countered by issuing a call to all citizens of the state between the ages of eighteen and forty-five to enroll in the state militia which he was organizing.[24] A few days later, on March 6, the McEnery forces attempted to capture the police stations in New Orleans but were repulsed. On the following day, the McEnery legislators were arrested and jailed,[25] bringing a temporary cessation to the Kellogg-McEnery hostilities. For the second time, Louisiana militiamen had been called up, and, as had been the case during its earlier mobilization, no real fighting had resulted.

Though the first two calls resulted in false alarms, the third one was to prove a charm. When the militia were next called up, they were to face a well-organized White League that was spoiling for a fight. The White League

[23] J. F. Casey to U. S. Grant, December 12, 1872, quoted in Warmoth, *War, Politics, and Reconstruction*, p. 217.
[24] Lonn, *Reconstruction in Louisiana*, p. 228.
[25] *American Annual Cyclopaedia, 1873*, p. 449.

grew out of a state-wide movement that enjoyed its greatest growth in the period from April to September, 1874. The first known league was formed in Opelousas in April of that year,[26] and the movement spread so rapidly that by August estimated membership was approximately 14,000.[27] Since the White Leagues are to be discussed in detail in Chapter IX, it need only be said here that they were in general politico-military organizations dedicated to the restoration of white supremacy by force if necessary. Only whites were allowed to join, and great emphasis was placed upon league members' being adequately armed and "prepared to meet any and every emergency."[28] In New Orleans, the Crescent City White League was formed in July, for "purely defensive" purposes it was claimed, and it was this particular group that was destined to clash with the state militia.

The immediate cause of the conflict was a dispute over the seizure of arms by the metropolitan police. During the month of August, 1874, several large shipments of arms reached New Orleans. These arms were undoubtedly distributed among the White Leaguers, and there was considerable boasting about the ultimate use to which the guns would be put.[29] On September 10, a detachment of policemen entered the Canal Street store of Arthur Olivier, an importer of firearms, placed him under arrest, and seized three cases of guns and twelve kegs of ammunition that had only recently arrived.[30] To judge from the reaction, this equipment was also scheduled for delivery to the Con-

[26] Fortier, *A History of Louisiana*, p. 135.

[27] Lonn, *Reconstruction in Louisiana*, p. 258.

[28] *Natchitoches* (La.) *Vindicator*, July 25, 1874, quoted in Lonn, *Reconstruction in Louisiana*, p. 259.

[29] Brewster, *Sketches*, p. 187.

[30] Fortier, *A History of Louisiana*, p. 138.

servatives. The act was condemned as "one of the most tyrannical and highhanded outrages which has yet disgraced the memory of freedom in this city," and many citizens complained that their constitutional right to bear arms was being infringed upon.[31]

The steamer *Mississippi* was scheduled to arrive in New Orleans on Monday, September 14, carrying another shipment of guns for the White League. When it was rumored about town that the police planned to seize the shipment, as they had already done in other instances, the White Leaguers called a protest meeting. In the September 13 newspapers appeared a statement to the "citizens of New Orleans" deploring the seizures and ending with the following appeal:[32]

We therefore call upon you on Monday morning, the 14th day of September, 1874, to close your places of business, without a single exception, and at eleven o'clock A.M. to assemble at the Clay statue on Canal Street, and in tones loud enough to be heard throughout the length and breadth of the land, Declare That You Are of Right, Ought To Be, And Mean To Be, Free.

In answer to the appeal, 3,000 to 5,000 citizens assembled on the proposed site at the scheduled hour. As the meeting progressed, it became apparent that the arms-bearing question had been lost in the larger political issues of the day, for the Kellogg-McEnery controversy was deliberately reopened. At the conclusion of a long address in which the speaker claimed that McEnery and Penn had really defeated Kellogg and Antoine and that the latter held office only through "fraud and violence," it was resolved that

[31] *New Orleans* (La.) *Picayune*, September 10, 1874, quoted in Lonn, *Reconstruction in Louisiana*, p. 269.

[32] *New Orleans* (La.) *Bulletin*, September 13, 1874, quoted in Fortier, *A History of Louisiana*, p. 139.

The Battle of New Orleans, September 14, 1874 (Harper's Weekly, 1874)

Kellogg should immediately resign. Five emissaries were sent to Kellogg to deliver the resolution, demand an immediate answer, then report his decision back to the meeting.[33]

The committee departed and called upon Kellogg but failed to see him personally. Henry C. Dibble, of Kellogg's staff, received the resolution and answered for the Governor, saying that no communication could be accepted while "large bodies of armed men" were assembled in the city.[34] When this information was repeated to the crowd, it was greeted with violent disapproval. Several fiery speeches were made, after which the men were instructed to go to their homes, get their arms, and report back at two-thirty in the afternoon ready for action. Since McEnery was out of the state, Lieutenant-Governor Penn issued a proclamation calling on the militia, "embracing all persons between the ages of eighteen and forty-five years, without regard to color or previous condition," to "arm and assemble for the purpose of driving the usurpers from power."[35] Penn then issued General Order 1 appointing Frederick Nash Ogden as provisional general of Louisiana State Militia.[36]

By three o'clock in the afternoon, the Conservatives had reassembled under arms. The first preparation for battle was to barricade the streets, a fitting manifestation of New Orleans' long-standing imitation of Parisian fashion. The situation grew tense; General Ogden, in command of a force composed primarily of New Orleans White Leaguers

[33] Brewster, *Sketches*, p. 191; Lonn, *Reconstruction in Louisiana*, p. 270; *Harper's Weekly*, October 3, 1874.

[34] H. C. Dibble to Committee, September 14, 1874, quoted in Fortier, *A History of Louisiana*, p. 143.

[35] Proclamation quoted in *ibid.*, pp. 145–46.

[36] *Ibid.*, p. 146.

disguised as a state militia, was opposed by the combined forces of Badger's metropolitan police and Longstreet's militia. Once again, General Emory and his regulars stood anxiously by.[37]

At about 4:15 P.M., Longstreet and Badger, with approximately 500 men, a Gatling gun, two 12-pound guns, and several other pieces of artillery, moved into position against the Ogden forces. Firing broke out on both sides shortly thereafter. A flanking movement by a company of Ogden's men followed by a frontal assault forced the metropolitans to fall back, abandoning their artillery to the enemy.[38] One participant claimed that General Longstreet "blanched" when he heard the White Leaguers give the rebel yell during their charge.[39] Longstreet received a minor wound, and General Badger was taken captive by his enemies after receiving three wounds, one of which necessitated a leg amputation.[40] On the following morning, the metropolitan police surrendered, as did the Negro militia stationed in the Statehouse. Kellogg retreated into the sanctity of the Custom House, and Penn took over the governorship pending McEnery's return to the state. The total number of casualties was estimated to be sixteen killed and forty-five wounded among the White Leaguers and eleven killed and sixty wounded among their opponents.[41]

Messages were immediately sent from Louisiana to influential persons in the North in an attempt to head off criticism of the revolutionary occurrences of September

[37] William H. Dixon, *White Conquest,* Vol. II, p. 25.
[38] F. N. Ogden to E. J. Ellis, September 17, 1874, quoted in Fortier, *A History of Louisiana,* pp. 148–53.
[39] Cited in Lonn, *Reconstruction in Louisiana,* p. 271.
[40] *New York Herald,* September 15, 1874.
[41] Fortier, *A History of Louisiana,* p. 153.

14. One nonparticipant asserted that he could easily understand "how hot-headed and imprudent men goaded as they are daily by Kellogg's seizures and illegal acts could not forego the opportunity. . . ."[42] Another more succinct account merely stated that "disgust . . . came to a head and like a huge boil burst."[43] Apparently the most influential message that left New Orleans was the one sent by the deposed Kellogg to President Grant seeking aid, for on September 15 the President issued a proclamation ordering "turbulent and disorderly persons," namely the Penn–Ogden–White League coalition, to "disperse and retire peaceably to their respective abodes within five days. . . ."[44] Additional federal troops and three naval vessels were ordered into New Orleans, and on September 19 Kellogg slipped back into the Statehouse, there to remain in uneasy residence for the remainder of his term.

The militia were to have yet another brief though anticlimactic period of activity in Louisiana. Following the election of 1876, the state was once again thrown into the unhappy situation of having two governors, when both Stephen B. Packard and Francis T. Nicholls claimed to have been elected. Packard, the Republican candidate, settled down in the Statehouse, derisively called "Fort Packard" by his enemies,[45] and issued the customary appeal to the President. However, events on the national scene regarding Hayes's election had caused a decided change in attitude on the Southern question. Grant, who

[42] G. Moorman to W. T. Sherman, September 15, 1874, William Tecumseh Sherman Papers.

[43] D. F. Boyd to W. T. Sherman, September 16, 1874, Sherman Papers.

[44] Richardson, *Messages of the Presidents*, pp. 276–77; *Harper's Weekly*, September 16, 1874.

[45] Lonn, *Reconstruction in Louisiana*, p. 487.

was operating only in a caretaker status until the inauguration of Hayes, notified Packard on March 1, 1877, that the military would no longer be used to maintain state administrations in Louisiana. On April 20, 1877, President Hayes issued the official order for the withdrawal of federal troops from New Orleans, and four days later the barracks were emptied. The Packard government, protected only by the Negro militia and remnants of the metropolitan police, dissolved immediately afterward, and Packard, claiming to have been "betrayed," departed for Liverpool, there to pacify himself with a consolation prize, an appointment as United States consul.[46]

Thereafter, the Negro militia movement in Louisiana came to an end. With the exception of the September 14 engagement, it was never a particularly active movement, and its lethargy was due to a combination of circumstances. In the first place, local Radicals were later in organizing their forces than their contemporaries in other Southern states. Too, since New Orleans was the seat of government, and since the troops were used almost exclusively in defense of incumbent administrations, militia activity was confined to that city alone and never spread to the provinces, as it did in other states. But by far the most important single factor that kept the Louisiana militia from engaging in little more than guard duty was the presence of appreciable numbers of Federal soldiers. Since they and not the militia were the prevailing force when a dispute arose, it was indeed fortunate for the militia that both groups championed identical causes until the very last.

[46] Garnie W. McGinty, *Louisiana Redeemed*, pp. 110, 121–23.

VI. Alarums and Excursions

RACE WAR WAS PERHAPS never so imminent in Mississippi as during the autumn of 1875. The condition of near-anarchy that accompanied almost any election in that state during Reconstruction was aggravated by the presence of two armed and hostile forces. One group was the Negro militia that had been called up by Governor Adelbert Ames in the wake of the slaughter at Clinton in September of that year; the other was the illegal white volunteer military force that had sprung up throughout the state as part of the Democratic program for victory in the coming election. Both sides were adequately armed and were busily engaged in the risky business of making frequent demonstrations of force in the face of the other. The air was heavy with threats and counterthreats, and active hostilities appeared inevitable. Both sides paraded through the streets accompanied by booming artillery salutes that kept tender nerves aquiver.[1] One eyewitness gave the following report of the situation in Jackson:[2]

I found the town in great excitement; ununiformed militia were parading the streets, both white and colored. I found that the white people—democrats—were very much excited in consequence of the governor organizing the militia force of the state. I found that he was about sending arms to Clinton and Edwards and other places along the line of the railroad. I found that these people were determined to resist his marching the militia to these points with arms, and that they threatened to kill his militiamen.

Outright war was avoided only by the complete surrender

[1] Paul Lewinson, *Race, Class, and Party*, p. 55.
[2] S. Rep. 527, 44th Cong., 1st Sess., p. 1801.

of one of the belligerents in the so-called "Peace Agreement" negotiated in October, 1875. In order to better understand the end of the story, it is necessary to reconstruct the sequence of events leading up to it.

On March 10, 1870, James L. Alcorn was inaugurated governor of Mississippi. In his inaugural address he urged citizens not to violate the laws or persecute other citizens. Although expressing a wish to avoid the cost of maintaining an armed militia, he gave fair warning that he would call up those forces if it became necessary to bring the people "to a sense of their obligations to society."[3] However, the fact that violence was held in check from 1871 to 1873 was due not primarily to fear of reprisal by the Governor but to a combination of peculiar local circumstances. In the first place, although Alcorn fell into disfavor with many persons because of his alleged defection into Republican ranks, he was never so bitterly resented by the Conservatives in Mississippi as was his successor, Northern-born Adelbert Ames, a former officer in the Union Army. It was almost inevitable that Alcorn, basically a Conservative in outlook, would eventually break with the Radical wing of his adopted party and find his way back into the Democratic fold (he was later prominent in helping draft the discriminatory constitution of 1890). Moreover, during this particular period both the internal weakness of the state Democratic party and the fear of federal intervention aided in keeping the peace.

In November, 1871, Alcorn resigned the governorship to succeed Hiram H. Revels in the United States Senate, and it was then that the split developed between him and Adelbert Ames, the other Senator from Mississippi. Both

---

[3] Garner, *Reconstruction in Mississippi*, p. 279.

men, seeking vindication from their constituents, entered the governor's race in the campaign of 1873. Ames headed the Radical faction of his own party, while Alcorn was supported by conservative Republicans and a not inconsiderable number of Democrats. When the vote was tallied, Ames was declared elected.

Dating from the defeat of Alcorn in 1873 and the subsequent increased numbers of Negro office holders,[4] the tempo of violence increased throughout the state, and Negro militia forces were called upon to play a more dominant role in political affairs. Several factors were responsible for the increasing unrest, chief among them being the intensity of feeling directed against Ames personally. He had come to Mississippi in 1866 in command of a detachment of federal troops assigned to garrison duty and had been appointed provisional governor by General Irwin McDowell in 1868, after the removal of Governor Benjamin G. Humphreys.[5] In March of the following year, he was given command of the entire Mississippi area and enjoyed the dual role of civil governor and military commander until the accession of Alcorn. In 1870, Ames beat his sword into a political plowshare and resigned from the Army. Along with Hiram Revels, he presented himself for acceptance to the United States Senate, where the irregularity of his credentials, which had been signed by Ames himself, caused a delay in his being seated. While he was in the Senate, his dedication to the advancement of the Negro race served only to widen the breach with the Conservatives back home. In

[4] Vernon L. Wharton, *The Negro in Mississippi, 1865–1890*, p. 182. (Hereafter cited as *The Negro in Mississippi*.)

[5] Percy L. Rainwater, ed., "The Autobiography of Benjamin Grubb Humphreys, August 26, 1808–December 20, 1882," *The Mississippi Valley Historical Review*, Vol. XXI (September, 1934), pp. 231–54.

addition to this, his political stature had not been enhanced on the local political scene by his marriage, which made him the son-in-law of Benjamin F. Butler.[6]

In addition to a personal dislike of Ames, two other factors contributed to an increase in violence. For one thing, the heretofore defunct Democratic party began to revive, and its recovery was attended by a growing emphasis on the use of force for political ends. At the same time, fear of federal intervention was on the wane; under the pressure of public opinion, the Grant administration was becoming more cautious in its Southern policy. At any rate, Ames was inaugurated on January 22, 1874, and before the year had run its course, the first outbreak occurred.

This conflict revolved about the figure of Peter Crosby, the Negro sheriff of Vicksburg. A "Taxpayers Convention," on December 6, 1874, demanded his resignation and, upon his refusal to comply, forcibly ejected him from office. Crosby immediately departed for Jackson, where he interviewed Governor Ames and received his promise of cooperation in retaking the office.[7] Hurrying back to Vicksburg, Crosby issued an appeal for all good Republicans to come to his assistance. Ames was as good as his word, and on December 4 he had his private secretary, A. G. Packer, who doubled as adjutant general of the state, send this message: "Captain P. C. Hall, care sheriff—cooperate with your militia company with Sheriff Crosby in his efforts to regain possession of his office. . . ."[8] Hall was the Negro captain of a seventy-five-man all-Negro company that had been organized in Vicksburg[9] and was at the time fully armed and

[6] For a concise account of Ames's personal and political career, see *Encyclopedia of Mississippi History*, Vol. I, pp. 84–109.

[7] Garner, *Reconstruction in Mississippi*, p. 329 *et passim*.

[8] Quoted in H.R. Rep. 265, 43d Cong., 2d Sess., p. xxv.

[9] *Ibid.*, p. iv.

equipped.[10] As Hall mobilized his forces, the situation grew tense. The mayor of Vicksburg, an anti-Ames man, issued a proclamation on December 7 closing all saloons, placed the city under martial law, and granted military command to a former Confederate officer with a force of 100 men.[11] Meanwhile, Crosby continued to recruit supporters from the outlying Negro settlements by circulating the story that both President Grant and Governor Ames were in Vicksburg and that to join the march on the city was the "Republican" thing to do.[12] Before the sun had set, the antagonists met in two separate battles; the latter was fought at the Pemberton monument, and resulted in the deaths of two whites and approximately thirty-six Negroes.[13] On December 21, President Grant issued a proclamation demanding the restoration of order, and on January 4, 1875, Governor Ames received this gratifying message from General Philip Sheridan: "I have tonight assumed control over the Department of the Gulf. A company of troops will be sent to Vicksburg tomorrow."[14]

Reaction to the Vicksburg riot was mixed. The local Conservatives went to the unnecessary trouble of electing another sheriff, only to see him deposed in mid-January by United States troops and the hated Crosby reinstated.[15] One Mississippian suggested that a double inscription be put on the Pemberton monument reading: "Here surrendered the Confederate chieftain in 1863, and here fell 100 Dupes to the unhallowed ambition of Adelbert Ames in

[10] Edward Mayes, *L. Q. C. Lamar, His Life, Times and Speeches*, p. 235. (Hereafter cited as *Lamar*.)

[11] Garner, *Reconstruction in Mississippi*, p. 329 *et passim*.

[12] *The Nation*, January 7, 1875.

[13] Garner, *Reconstruction in Mississippi*, p. 329 *et passim*.

[14] Philip H. Sheridan to Adelbert Ames, January 4, 1875, Philip Sheridan Papers.

[15] Garner, *Reconstruction in Mississippi*, p. 329 *et passim*.

1874."[16] The Northern press voiced a slightly different view:[17]

The latest outbreak of negrophobia has occurred in Mississippi, in Vicksburg, and with more disastrous results than have usually attended these terrible evidences of an irreconcilable antagonism of races. . . . It was, in fact, from the Vicksburgian point of view nothing but a quiet little affair in which seventy colored citizens were murdered in cold blood and one white citizen had lost his valuable life. . . .

Once more, as always, it is the negroes that are slaughtered, while the whites escape.

After the trouble in Vicksburg, Ames sought to strengthen his position. In a message to the Legislature, he decried the lack of a "well organized or disciplined militia" and reminded the lawmakers that even if such men were available he did not have "a dollar to expend" for such a purpose.[18] Veering sharply away from his earlier desultory enforcement policies, he threw his weight behind a metropolitan-police bill designed to create the hard core of a loyal army.[19] Although this move was defeated, he refused to give up, and on February 25 he managed to push through the Legislature an act disbanding existing militia companies, revoking previously issued commissions, and requiring state arms to be turned in.[20] By this measure he hoped not only to curb the growing white rifle companies that were multiplying throughout the state but also to regain possession of state arms for reissue to a reinvigorated

[16] Charles Furlong, *Origin of the Outrages at Vicksburg*, p. 16.

[17] *The Independent*, December 17, 1874.

[18] Message to Legislature, December 17, 1874, quoted in J. S. McNeily, "Climax and Collapse of Reconstruction in Mississippi, 1874–1896," *Publications of the Mississippi Historical Society*, Vol. XII (1912), p. 325.

[19] Garner, *Reconstruction in Mississippi*, pp. 327–28.

[20] Mayes, *Lamar*, p. 239.

militia. His hopes were foiled again, largely because the act was ignored by those in possession of the arms. However, continued pressure by the Governor led to the passage in the spring of 1875 of what became known as the "Gatling Gun Bill," which authorized the governor to organize two regiments of ten companies each and appropriated $60,000 for that purpose. Of this money, $5,000 was to be used for the purchase of arms, including Gatling guns.[21]

With this law safely on the statute books, Ames, either lulled into a false sense of security or fearful of creating a race war, took no action to organize his militia when the campaign of 1875 approached. Unfortunately for the Governor, he apparently failed to comprehend the earnestness with which the Mississippi Democrats determined to regain control of the state. While he continued to hope for a free ballot and a fair election, his opponents were perfecting their quasi-military organization, which would later serve as a blueprint for the technique in political violence known as the "Shotgun Plan." It was no mere coincidence that the Democrats selected as their campaign manager James Z. George, an attorney experienced in military as well as political affairs. He personally conducted the subsequent campaign, which set a new high in frenzied eruptions of political violence.

The first and mildest of the disturbances associated with the campaign took place in Vicksburg on July 4, 1875, some three months before the election. The Negroes held a meeting at the courthouse "for the performance of patriotic exercises," in which the scheduled speaker was T. W. Cardoza, perhaps the most bitterly hated of Mississippi's Negro politicians. An altercation between Cardoza and a local judge resulting from an unflattering editorial

[21] Garner, *Reconstruction in Mississippi*, p. 382.

—"The negroes of the South are free—free as air," says the parliamentary Watterson. This is what the *State*, a well-known Democratic organ of Tennessee, says, in huge capitals, on the subject: "Let it be known before the election that the leaders have agreed to spot every leading Radical negro in the county, and treat him as an enemy for all time to come. The rotten ring must and shall be broken at any and all costs. The Democrats have determined to withdraw all employment from their enemies. Let this fact be known."

"OF COURSE HE WANTS TO VOTE THE DEMOCRATIC TICKET!"

DEMOCRATIC "REFORMER." "You're as free as air, ain't you? Say you are, or I'll blow yer black head off!"

Basic element of the "Shotgun Plan": Political intimidation of the Southern Negro (Harper's Week-

written by Cardoza led to a general outbreak, during which several Negroes were killed.[22]

Peace had hardly returned to the countryside when another and more violent outbreak occurred in Yazoo City. Conditions in that delta town had remained agitated because of the activities of A. T. Morgan, the Republican sheriff. Morgan, a carpetbag-planter turned politician, had previously been involved in a Yazoo City murder, having shot the man whose job he subsequently filled. In addition, he had committed the social indiscretion of marrying a Negro schoolmistress, an act that did nothing to increase his popularity in local white circles.[23] On September 1, 1875, a political meeting was held in Bedwell's Hall with Morgan as the featured speaker. The meeting was attended by a group of Democrats who interrupted and heckled Morgan as he tried to speak. An argument followed, whereupon pistols were drawn and the hall took on the appearance of a shooting gallery.[24] One white man and three Negroes were killed, and the city was immediately placed under martial law.[25] According to the *Yazoo Banner*, Morgan "hastened to Cassius Ames to whom he cries to help him, ere he sinks."[26] Ames threatened to restore Morgan by returning him with an escort of 300 Negro militiamen but was persuaded to change his plan when he learned that the people of Yazoo City had assembled under arms to resist any such maneuver and were threatening to hang

[22] S. Rep. 527, Vol. I, 44th Cong., 1st Sess., p. lxi; *Encyclopedia of Mississippi History*, Vol. I, p. 100.

[23] S. Rep. 527, Vol. I, 44th Cong., 1st Sess., p. lxi.

[24] A. T. Morgan to A. Ames, September 4, 1875, Adelbert Ames Papers. Morgan wrote Ames a fifty-odd-page report of the Yazoo City riot.

[25] Garner, *Reconstruction in Mississippi*, p. 375.

[26] Cited in Morgan, *Yazoo*, pp. 468–69.

Morgan and kill every Negro militiaman.[27] Morgan discreetly decided to remain in Jackson under the protective wing of the Governor.

Before the Yazoo City dead were decently buried, the worst of the pre-election riots broke out in the Baptist-seminary town of Clinton, only a few miles from the state capital. At a political meeting and barbecue held in Clinton on September 4, it was planned to allow both Democrats and Republicans to speak. Before the meeting, the Republicans staged a demonstration in which 800 Negroes, armed and organized into a cavalry company, rode through the streets of the town on gaily beribboned horses, followed by several more companies afoot.[28] Later in the day, while a Republican named Fisher was attempting to address the crowd, a fight broke out nearby between a white man and a Negro over a bottle of whisky. A shot was fired, and in the melee that followed, three whites were killed and several others wounded.[29] When word of this incident spread, armed groups of whites from Jackson, Vicksburg, and Edwards Station rushed to Clinton by special train bent on revenge.[30] For nearly two days, this mob combed the surrounding area indiscriminately shooting and killing an estimated twenty to thirty Negroes. Many Negroes fled to Jackson seeking the Governor's aid and protection, while others "hid out" in the woods, struck "with a terror not easily described."[31]

The Governor issued a proclamation on September 7

[27] S. Rep. 527, Vol. I, 44th Cong., 1st Sess., p. lxii; testimony of G. K. Chase, *ibid.*, p. 1803.

[28] Charles H. Brough, "The Clinton Riot," *Publications of the Mississippi Historical Society*, Vol. VI (1902), p. 56.

[29] S. Rep. 527, Vol. I, 44th Cong., 1st Sess., p. lxiii–lxiv.

[30] Garner, *Reconstruction in Mississippi*, p. 378.

[31] T. Dabney to E. Dabney, October 20, 1875, quoted in Susan D. Smedes, *A Southern Planter*, p. 232.

against "persons in various parts of the state" who had formed themselves into military companies and commanded them to disband immediately.[32] His order was openly defied, and the *Yazoo City Herald* made this bitter retort:[33]

Our dapper little Governor Ames comes to the front with a proclamation ordering the disbandment of all military companies now organized in the state. If he has brains enough to know his right hand from his left, he ought to know that no more attention will be paid to his proclamation than the moon is popularly supposed to pay to the baying of a sheep-killing dog.

While his opponents were defiant, his supporters were worried. Letters such as the following poured into the Governor's office describing the chaotic conditions that existed throughout the state:[34]

To Excellency Gov. Ames:

The rebels turbulent; are arming themselves here now today to go up to Sartartia to murder more poor negroes. Gov., aint the no pertection? This confederate military all over the state, now called Granger. They are better prepared now for fighting than they was before the war. The read yr proclamation today and damn you and proclamation too; they intend to hang you ore get some secret scoundral to kill you. . . .

These unsettled conditions caused Ames to turn to the federal government for aid. On September 8, he appealed to President Grant for troops to restore order in Mississippi. General George, directing Democratic strategy, simultaneously telegraphed Washington insisting that

---

[32] S. Rep. 527, Vol. I, 44th Cong., 1st Sess., p. xii.
[33] Quoted in Morgan, *Yazoo*, p. 470.
[34] Letter to Ames signed "We colored citizens" of Vicksburg, September 8, 1875, quoted in S. Rep. 527, Vol. II, 44th Cong., 1st Sess., p. 89.

"peace prevails."[35] On September 14, Grant, through his Attorney General, refused Ames's request and declared that "the whole public are tired of the annual autumnal outbreaks in the south."[36] Ames was now left to his own devices.

Pressure began to mount favoring effective organization of the Negro militia. Ames continued to fret over the possibility of drifting into race war, and as late as September 11 he voiced his opposition to a "militia of colored men,"[37] fearing that such action would develop into "a war of races which would extend beyond the borders of this state."[38] More and louder demands for the militia were heard as the trouble within the state continued. The Governor's close political advisers favored the move, hoping it would be possible to "preserve the peace with these men."[39] Even the Northern press joined the hue and cry against Ames, calling him "a mere sham" and demanding to know the whereabouts of the state militia.[40] Thus Ames, harassed by the internal conditions of the state, abandoned by the federal government, and influenced by the advice of his nearest and most trusted friends, began to act.

On September 24, Adjutant General Packer sent the following message to every sheriff in the state: "Sir: I am directed by his excellency the governor to inquire if any militia organizations are needed in your county to

[35] Garner, *Reconstruction in Mississippi*, p. 380.

[36] Cited in Wharton, *The Negro in Mississippi*, p. 194.

[37] A. Ames to A. T. Morgan, August 14, 1874, Ames Papers.

[38] Telegram from Governor Ames to Attorney General Edwards Pierrepont, September 11, 1875, quoted in Garner, *Reconstruction in Mississippi*, pp. 382–83.

[39] Charles W. Clarke to A. Ames, September 16, 1875, quoted in S. Rep. 527, Vol. II, 44th Cong., 1st Sess., p. 92.

[40] *The Independent*, September 16, 1875.

assist the civil officers? Are there any threats from the opposition that in your judgment, will be carried into effect? . . ."[41] Responses to this feeler were varied. Some sheriffs definitely wanted militia, others did not. Most reluctant of those contacted was the sheriff of Pike County: "I intend to do all in my power to preserve the peace and make arrests without bringing about conflict. And when it comes to that, I shall think it my first duty to keep out of it. . . . Our party is not composed of fighting material."[42] But Ames was not deterred from his course, for on the last day of September he wrote President Grant: "I am organizing the militia and will fight . . . if necessary."[43]

Though the Governor called up what he described as "the only available force, the colored militia,"[44] he confined these troops primarily to the area around Jackson. The Negro companies were composed chiefly of refugees from the recent Clinton riot and were under the leadership of a fiery mulatto, Charles Caldwell.[45] In an effort to train and equip his forces, Ames ordered 100 copies of Upton's *Infantry Tactics* from a New York publisher, 1,000 Springfield rifles, 1,500 haversacks, and 5,000 rations of pork and bacon.[46] These warlike preparations

[41] Cited in S. Rep. 527, Vol. I, 44th Cong., 1st Sess., p. lxviii.

[42] McNeily, "Climax and Collapse of Reconstruction in Mississippi, 1874–1896," p. 146.

[43] Adelbert Ames to Ulysses S. Grant, September 30, 1875, Ames Papers.

[44] Adelbert Ames to James W. Garner, January 17, 1900, James W. Garner Papers.

[45] Frank Johnston, "The Conference of October 15, 1875, between General George and Governor Ames," *Publications of the Mississippi Historical Society*, Vol. VI (1902), p. 67; S. Rep. 527, Vol. I, 44th Cong., 1st Sess., p. lxx. Garner, *Reconstruction in Mississippi*, p. 382. *Hinds County* (Miss.) *Gazette*, September 29, 1875.

[46] Garner, *Reconstruction in Mississippi*, p. 382; S. Rep. 527, Vol. I, 44th Cong., 1st Sess., p. lxix.

caused an immediate reaction. The Conservatives loudly protested that the Governor's action was unconstitutional[47] and charged that he was deliberately bringing about a war between the races.[48] The usually eloquent L. Q. C. Lamar was plunged into despair over the future of Mississippi: "Ames has it dead. There can be no escape from his rule. His negro regiments are nothing. He will get them killed up and then Grant will take possession for him."[49] The *Jackson Vindicator* made the following analysis of the situation: "The organization of militia companies still goes bravely on. Jackson's sons with Jackson's guns will fight for Jackson's glory. All this seems like preparing for war, but not so; only preparing to attack $60,000.00 of the people's money in the state treasury. . . ."[50] A more extreme reaction came in the form of anonymous threats, such as the following:[51]

A. Ames

The White Leaguers of Claiborne have determined to get rid of J. J. Smith . . . and other scallawags in this county. Our brothers in your section will look after you. Send out your negro troops and Gatlin guns, and we will wipe them from the face of the earth, which they disgrace. We have the best rifles, and [are] eager for an opportunity to use them.

In early October, 1875, the last concentrated outbreak of violence took place in northwest Mississippi, at Friar's Point, the home of former Governor James L. Alcorn, in Coahoma County. Alcorn, now gravitating back to-

---

[47] *Jackson* (Miss.) *Weekly Clarion*, October 13, 1875.
[48] S. Rep. 527, Vol. I, 44th Cong., 1st Sess., p. lxxi; Garner, *Reconstruction in Mississippi*, p. 383.
[49] Mayes, *Lamar*, p. 211.
[50] Quoted in *Hinds County* (Miss.) *Gazette*, September 29, 1875.
[51] Quoted in S. Rep. 527, Vol. I, 44th Cong., 1st Sess., p. 26.

ward his original political position, had allied himself with the Conservatives in that county and had led in denouncing the local Radical group headed by Sheriff Brown. Alcorn made a speech accusing Brown of being a defaulter.[52] When the sheriff prepared to answer the charge, Alcorn let it be known that he would personally attend the speech "at all hazards" because of Brown's "habit of denouncing me [Alcorn] with all the vulgarity . . . possible." Brown thereupon sent messengers into the surrounding countryside to bring in an armed force to protect him "in his right to speak," and on the following Tuesday several hundred armed Negroes marched toward the town. The white company in Friar's Point sent a messenger to the advancing column ordering them to disperse within fifteen minutes or risk attack. After a hasty consultation, the Negro force retreated a mile or so away from town to await reinforcements.[53] Because of the threatening nature of the situation, the women and children were evacuated from Friar's Point and sent across the river to Helena, Arkansas, where a volunteer company was raised and sent to Alcorn's aid. The whites decided to attack before enemy reinforcements could arrive, and, in spite of their expressed intention to fire over the Negroes' heads, eight persons were killed in the fray. The Negroes were dispersed, and Brown later turned up in Memphis with the explanation that he had been "detached from his friends early in the trouble."[54]

Reports from other sections of the state showed that conditions were uniformly agitated. Less than a week

[52] *New York Herald*, October 6, 1875.
[53] S. Rep. 527, Vol. I, 44th Cong., 1st Sess., pp. 69–70.
[54] *New York Herald*, October 6, 7, 1875.

THE MISSISSIPPI LEGISLATURE HAS KILLED ITSELF BY WITHDRAWING THE IMPEACHMENT, AND THE GOVERNOR HAS KILLED HIMSELF BY RESIGNING HIS OFFICE

KILLING POLITE.

Resignation of Governor Adelbert Ames, of Mississippi   (Harper's Weekly, 1876)

after the Friar's Point affair, Ames received this letter from Vicksburg:[55]

Governor Ames:
Dear Sir: I think this morning that you ought to be notified how things are going on in Warren County around Vicksburg. Ever since Sat the democrat party has been like roaring lions; they have sworn to not let us colored militia organize in this city, and been going every since Sat night with their guns— going round the halls to see if any of them are gathered to- gether, to break them up, and making their threats what they intend to do with the governor; that if he sends Chas. Caldwell down to Vicksburg with guns and ammunition to arm the ne- groes, that he will never get there. . . . An extra train leaving here in the morning for Jackson, who supposed to be the leading tigers of this city, going out to make Governor Ames call in them arms and disband that negro militia. . . .

Meanwhile, in Jackson, where Ames had placed sev- eral Negro companies on a war footing, danger of an out- break increased hourly. Parading companies of armed whites and Negroes furnished a handy excuse for con- flict. Excitement had reached fever point and bloodshed seemed inevitable, when on October 15, 1875, the adver- saries negotiated a "Peace Agreement," which proved to be the undoing of the Governor. The agreement was reached largely through the influence of G. K. Chase, "a gentleman of intelligence and good address," who had been sent to Mississippi by Attorney General Edwards Pierrepont to report on the true condition of affairs there.[56] Chase was instrumental in bringing representatives of both groups together, and a committee headed by Gen-

[55] Anonymous letter to Adelbert Ames, October 13, 1875, quoted in S. Rep. 527, Vol. II, 44th Cong., 1st Sess., p. 85.
[56] A. J. Brown, *A History of Newton County*, p. 184.

eral George called upon the Governor in an effort to work
out details of a compromise.[57] The committee suggested
that the best way to settle the unrest in the state would
be to disband the militia; Ames countered by proposing
to disband them but to allow them to keep their guns.
This was objected to on the grounds that such action
would "be the source of serious disturbances," and the
final decision was to deposit the arms with the commander
of federal troops stationed in Jackson.[58] The general terms
of agreement were that Ames would disband the militia
in exchange for assurances of a peaceful and orderly election.[59]

The announcement of the compromise was greeted with
varied reactions. Generally, the press applauded the sus-
pension of military operations,[60] but such sentiment was
by no means unanimous. The editor of *The Nation*, for
example, remarked with some acerbity that the "spirit of
concord" in all probability resulted from the fact "the
gunpowder had given out."[61] One perturbed Mississippian
came uncomfortably close to truth when he remarked
that "J. Z. George and Co. Hoodwinked the President of
U. S. about Peace in Miss. Election."[62]

The "Peace Agreement" was disastrous to the Republicans for two very good reasons. In the first place, it left
them defenseless in the face of an armed and pitiless ad-
versary, and, in the second place, the Democrats deliberately avoided living up to their end of the bargain. By

---

[57] Garner, *Reconstruction in Mississippi*, pp. 387–88.
[58] James D. Lynch, *Kemper County Vindicated, and a Peep at
Radical Rule in Mississippi*, p. 300.
[59] Garner, *Reconstruction in Mississippi*, p. 388.
[60] *New York Herald*, October 16, 1875.
[61] *The Nation*, October 28, 1875.
[62] J. Meek to Adelbert Ames, November 2, 1875, Ames Papers.

a calculated program of fraud, violence, and intimidation, the Democrats won an overwhelming victory in the election of November 3. As soon as the new legislature convened, the first order of business was to draw up articles of impeachment against Ames, who, by yet another compromise, was allowed to resign the governorship.

The election of 1875, which marked the return to power of the Democrats in Mississippi, marked the end of Negro militia in that state. No one can say what the results might have been if Ames had been willing to use, rather than merely organize, his Negro troops. This much, however, is certain. The governor should never have organized them unless he intended to put them to use, because from the moment mobilization began, they became targets for a well-armed enemy. Ames's half-measures, all sound and no fury, in regard to the Negro militia, paint him in unflattering and uninspiring colors as a timid Caesar, unwilling to cross the Rubicon.

VII.   Life in the Militia

A SOLDIER, LIKE ANY OTHER MAN, is vitally affected by the milieu in which he must function. The relentless pressure of existing circumstances was continually at work on the militia forces, and a knowledge of internal conditions does much to explain not only what they accomplished but also what they failed to accomplish.

In the course of their existence, militia units generally passed through two distinct and dissimilar phases. The first was the period of organization, when enthusiasm was extremely high and participation in the movement was merely an extension of the social and political life of the community. The second phase began when the unit was called up for active service. During military operations, militiamen came face to face with the less attractive features of soldiering. The physical discomforts and material inconveniences of camp life were aggravated by the uneven administration of military discipline. The joy previously shown on the parade ground disappeared in the face of long and extended marches through the countryside, while both the pleasure and the security of being under arms were dampened by the sporadic outbreaks of violence that took the lives of many of their troops. Since militiamen were generally lacking in any fundamental military training or indoctrination, it is not surprising that morale and discipline practically disappeared.

Enthusiasm reached its highest point during the period when the units were being molded into shape. This was due to the novelty of the experience and also to the fact that the Negro felt that by joining up he was somehow participating in a crusade on his own behalf. There were several other very concrete attractions that helped keep him interested in and proud of his unit. For one thing, militia activity was oftentimes tied directly to the social life of the community. Militia captains, for example, enjoyed an enviable position in the social hierarchy and were very much in demand at local functions. Musters and drills furnished welcome relief from the boredom of routine plantation life. Recreation and entertainment came to be closely associated with militia exercises. Pleasure trips and picnics were frequently scheduled, and special occasions were commemorated by some more spectacular activity, such as competitive target-shooting.[1] Political campaigns, as well as social affairs, were also allied with militia organizations and their activities. Military parades in support of Republican candidates were quite common and were usually followed by gigantic barbecues, where all those present could feast not only on spareribs but also on the bombastic orations of political hopefuls.

Another reason for the Negro's early enthusiasm for the militia was his delight in the trappings of military life. The pay was a welcome augmentation to the small income of the average agricultural worker (the overwhelming majority of Negro militiamen seem to have been recruited from the plantations), and the fact that he enjoyed his military duties caused him to look on his salary as being in the nature of a windfall. Too, he undoubtedly experienced much gratification in wearing the uniform of his state militia. The laxity of uniform regulations allowed considerable freedom in the matter of military dress, with the result that many outfits were extremely colorful. Ned Tennant, leader of the Edgefield, South Carolina, militia unit, dec-

---

[1] Testimony of Doc Adams, S. Misc. Doc. 48, Vol. I, 44th Cong., 2d Sess., p. 49. Adams was captain of the militia company that was later annihilated at Hamburg, South Carolina.

Fourth of July Parade, 1876 (Harper's Weekly, 1876)

orated his uniform with a long ostrich plume.[2] Oliver Cromwell, who led the huge Negro parade in Clinton, Mississippi, before the riot of September, 1875, wore a plumed hat and cavalry saber and sat astride a horse trimmed in red, white, and blue ribbons.[3] In addition to his satisfaction with the pay and the uniform, the Negro dearly loved the gun issued to him by the state. In some cases, it was the first firearm ever possessed by the freedman, and in almost all cases it was the finest he had ever had. He quickly demonstrated an aptitude for marksmanship.

These were the factors that were responsible for the early flush of enthusiasm for the militia. Because participation in the social and political life of the community plus the personal satisfactions derived from military ritual impressed him favorably, the Negro soldier was happy, loyal to his command, proud of his unit, and eager to attend drills and musters.

Disillusionment set in when the militia was placed on a war footing. Mobilization was almost always accompanied by a gradual deterioration of morale. Time and again, commanders in the field complained of the "demoralized and very unsatisfactory condition" of their troops.[4] As morale continued to drop, the thin layer of military varnish wore away, while at the same time even the most rudimentary forms of discipline were forgotten or ignored. Subsequent results were disastrous to the militia. Equipment issued by the state was inadequately or improperly cared for. Guns were lost, misplaced, or stolen,[5] and little effort was wasted

---

[2] Simkins, *Pitchfork Ben Tillman*, p. 59.

[3] C. H. Brough, "The Clinton Riot," p. 56.

[4] *Annual Report of the Adjutant General of the State of Louisiana, 1874*, p. 3.

[5] K. Danforth to Lt. —. —. Gibbons, June 25, 1869, AGO files, state of Arkansas.

on cleaning and oiling the weapons.[6] Uniforms were arbitrarily altered to suit the sartorial tastes of the wearer, with cavalier indifference to such regulations as existed. So general did this practice become that in some areas changing the shape or style of the uniform was made a court-martial offense.[7] Selling or pawning of military gear in order to raise cash for immediate and generally non-military purposes became standard procedure, and steps had to be taken to prevent disposition of state-owned clothing for personal gain. In Tennessee, periodic inspections and inventories were prescribed,[8] while in Louisiana uniforms were kept under lock and key in the state armory and were issued only on days when they were actually needed.[9]

Equally serious was the progressive tendency to violate the chain of command. Officers experienced increasing difficulty in enforcing discipline, and disobedience of orders was a common charge in military trials.[10] Threats against officers' lives were not unheard of, and cases of actual mutiny were reported.[11] Life within the camp was not unaffected by these conditions. Thefts of personal and state property were common. Fist fights and other forms of

[6] Report of the Inspector General, Louisiana State Militia, January 6, 1871, quoted in *Annual Report of the Adjutant General of the State of Louisiana, 1870*, p. 21.

[7] General Order 3, February 6, 1874, quoted in *Annual Report of the Adjutant General of the State of Louisiana, 1874*, p. 38.

[8] General Joseph Cooper to Col. —. —. Gamble, March 13, 1869, AGO files, state of Tennessee.

[9] General Order 15, May 29, 1874, quoted in *Annual Report of the Adjutant General of the State of Louisiana, 1874*, p. 48.

[10] General Order 11, General Order Book, Tennessee State Guards, 1869, AGO files, state of Tennessee.

[11] During the period of martial law in Arkansas in 1868–69, the Negro troops under General Mallory rebelled and threatened his life. So explosive was the situation that the Negro troops were disbanded. (Harrell, *The Brooks and Baxter War*, p. 87.)

rowdyism frequently broke out, and drunkenness became a problem of some magnitude.[12]

Disaffection and dissatisfaction found a ready outlet in desertion. In one company, there were fourteen desertions during a ten-day period, and thirty Tennessee guards deserted in a body.[13] Defection was deliberately encouraged by the whites in an attempt to place the militia in an unfavorable light. In South Carolina, opponents of the militia offered Negroes seventy-five cents a day plus rations, with a promise of steady employment, if they would desert.[14] Militia captains were forced to take extreme measures to combat this situation. One Tennessean was ridden out of town on a rail in punishment for inciting troops to desert.[15]

Several attempts were made to improve conditions within the militia, in hopes of halting the disintegration of morale and discipline. General Longstreet requested a revision of the Louisiana militia law as the first step toward a reinvigorated force. Stressing the harmful effects resulting from delay in payment of troops, he proposed abolishing several restrictions.[16] Another prominent general felt that the problem could be solved through a weeding-out process and argued in favor of "one good full regiment of well-drilled, efficient, reliable troops . . . in place of a brigade on paper."[17] Still another maneuver to improve

[12] Regimental Order 3, February 23, 1869, General Order Book, Tennessee State Guards, 1869, AGO files, state of Tennessee.

[13] Captain —. —. Clingan to General Joseph Cooper, July 11, 1869, AGO files, state of Tennessee; *Nashville* (Tenn.) *Union and Dispatch*, September 17, 1867.

[14] R. B. Elliott to R. K. Scott, September 13, 1869. Military Affairs File, state of South Carolina.

[15] *Nashville* (Tenn.) *Union and Dispatch*, June 1, 1867.

[16] *Annual Report of the Adjutant General of the State of Louisiana, 1870*, p. 5.

[17] *Annual Report of the Adjutant General of the State of Louisiana, 1874*, p. 4.

morale was the granting of preferential treatment to militiamen by allowing them exemption from jury duty and from a specified amount of taxation in return for faithful service.[18]

A more direct approach was adopted to meet the problems of drunkenness and rowdyism. In an effort to keep the soldiers from obtaining whisky, proclamations of this nature were posted by commanders: "Any citizen who shall sell or give any intoxicating beverage to any officer or enlisted man of this command will have his place of business closed up and will be arrested and severely punished."[19] Rowdyism led to an increased emphasis on discipline, claiming that a "non-disciplined militia establishes a false idea of the duties of a soldier and makes the force entirely useless,"[20] officers attempted to take up the slack. A new severity of tone crept into published orders threatening trial by "drum-head court martial" and prompt punishment.[21] When all else failed, there was recourse to military law. Court-martial boards were constantly being called into session to hear cases and pass judgments. Punishment varied with the offense committed; those found guilty of minor violations were assigned extra hours of duty with the camp labor force,[22] while more serious convictions re-

[18] Recommended by the inspector general of the Louisiana State Militia in the annual report of January 6, 1871 (*Annual Report of the Adjutant General of the State of Louisiana, 1870*, p. 22). He claimed that "by these means, the militia will always be kept up to a proper standard and composed of the right class of men."

[19] Post Order 3, February 26, 1869, General Order Book, Tennessee State Guards, 1869, AGO files, state of Tennessee.

[20] *Annual Report of the Adjutant General of the State of Louisiana, 1874*, p. 5.

[21] General Order 4, Tennessee State Guards, February 23, 1869, quoted in S. Rep. 21, Part 1, 42d Cong., 2d Sess., p. 460.

[22] General Order 11, General Order Book, Tennessee State Guards, 1869, AGO files, state of Tennessee.

sulted in such penalties as reduction in rank, fines, dishonorable discharge, and, in isolated cases, death, as, for example, when militiamen in Arkansas were convicted of rape (see Chapter III).

It can scarcely be claimed that justice was administered in an evenhanded fashion, since the severity of the punishment varied from place to place. For example, a Tennessee private found guilty of desertion was subjected to the humiliation of being "dishonorably drummed out of camp and the service of the State of Tennessee with one side of his head shorn and [his] right breast bearing the inscription Deserter in large and plain characters [and] marched to the tune of the Rogue's March escorted by a guard [to] at least one mile from camp."[23]

On the other hand, a lieutenant in the Louisiana Militia was found guilty of the impressive charges of "mutiny, insubordination, disobedience of orders, neglect of duty, contempt and disrespect to superior officers, conduct prejudicial to good order and discipline [and] conduct unbecoming an officer and a gentleman," yet his sentence was merely "to be reprimanded in General Orders."[24]

In this survey of the two distinct phases through which militia units passed, one is struck by the invariable change from enthusiasm and interest to disaffection and dissolution. There were several basic reasons for the drastic reduction in effectiveness. One was the inferior quality of the officer corps. Although some officers were both competent and conscientious, the over-all level was very low indeed, resulting from the fact that most of them either

[23] Order of March 4, 1869, issued by Colonel —. —. Gamble, AGO files, state of Tennessee.

[24] General Order 27, October 8, 1874, *Annual Report of the Adjutant General of the State of Louisiana, 1874*, p. 56.

were political appointees or had been elected by the men,
usually without regard for ability or for past experience.
The officers' lack of interest was reflected in their failure
to uniform or arm themselves properly or to attend drills
and musters regularly. Twenty-three commissions in the
Louisiana Militia were revoked at one time on these
grounds.[25] Unauthorized absences from command also
gave cause for concern,[26] and charges of neglect of duty
were common, especially when forces were in the field.[27]
Violations of even the most elementary code of military
conduct were responsible for many courts-martial, where
"drunkenness and conduct unbecoming an officer and a
gentleman" were common charges.[28] Lieutenant E. K.
Brown, of the Tennessee State Guards, was tried on the
dual charges of "habitual drunkenness and utter worth-
lessness,"[29] while Captain S. L. Chambers was dishonorably discharged from service for getting drunk, threatening civilians with his pistol, and using obscene language.[30]

These, of course, were extreme cases, but there is considerable evidence that improvement among officer personnel was sorely needed. The inspector-general of the
Louisiana Militia declared that "company officers seem
to have lost their energy and ambition" and complained

[25] *Annual Report of the Adjutant General of the State of Louisiana, 1874*, p. 60.
[26] In Tennesee, General Joseph Cooper issued a circular warning officers against this practice. Copy of circular in AGO file, state of Tennessee.
[27] General Order 13, August 24 1867, General Order Book, Tennessee State Guards, 1867, AGO files, state of Tennessee.
[28] This charge appears more frequently than any other in the court-martial records.
[29] General Order 12, August 21, 1867, General Order Book, Tennessee State Guards, 1867, AGO files, state of Tennessee.
[30] Colonel —. —. Gamble to General Joseph Cooper, July 14, 1867, AGO files, state of Tennessee.

that "the whole command is . . . demoralized." He insisted that "competent officers" were needed throughout the entire force.[31] Another general reported to his superiors: "The officers in this brigade are inefficient and incompetent to a degree that constrains me to request that they be ordered before a Board of Examinations to pass upon the question of their fitness for the positions which they now hold."[32]

Another factor contributing to the lowering of morale in the militia was the haphazard manner of paying off the troops. As in any army in any age, the soldiers looked forward to payday and its attendant pleasures. Anger and dissatisfaction were immediately voiced when the occasion was overlooked. This problem repeatedly arose in Louisiana, Arkansas, and Tennessee. Longstreet specifically urged that his troops must be paid more promptly in the interest of efficiency.[33] Quite often wages were long overdue. One field officer of the Tennessee State Guards complained that his men had "over five months [pay] due them,"[34] and the adjutant general of Arkansas wrote a letter to each member of the Legislature urging them to appropriate money to pay the troops for services rendered a year earlier.[35] The failure of the paymaster to settle arrears undoubtedly contributed to the desertions, which increased at an alarming rate.[36] A company in Edgefield,

[31] Report dated January 6, 1871, quoted in *Annual Report of the Adjutant General of the State of Louisiana, 1870*, p. 21.

[32] General Frank Morey to General Henry Street, December 1, 1874, quoted in *Annual Report of the Adjutant General of the State of Louisiana, 1874*, p. 19.

[33] *Annual Report of the Adjutant General of the State of Louisiana, 1870*, p. 5.

[34] Major —. —. Robeson to General Joseph Cooper, December 14, 1867, AGO files, state of Tennessee.

[35] Copy of letter dated June 1, 1870, in the possession of the author.

[36] *Nashville* (Tenn.) *Union and Dispatch*, September 17, 1867.

South Carolina, threatened to disband unless they were paid their due,[37] and commanders continually protested to legislators that until the militia forces were properly cared for by the state "they will exist simply in name and remain practically a farce."[38]

Perhaps no other influence was so demoralizing as the poor conditions under which militiamen lived when they were called into active service. The failure of the quartermasters to provide for the forces resulted in part from the methods under which they were forced to operate. Logistic support, except for the single category of arms and ammunition, was accomplished by empowering the quartermaster-general "to impress such stores, supplies and buildings for quarters as may be required."[39] The troops lived off the countryside, commandeering supplies from inhabitants for which they gave receipts promising future payment.[40] Such irregular methods were generally ineffective, and living conditions thus left much to be desired. Although every army complains about its food, justifiable protests were heard from militiamen from time to time. Troopers complained about the "irregular manner" in which they received their rations and were particularly vociferous whenever denied "an allowance of coffee, sugar and other necessaries pertaining to a soldier's allowance."[41] One private wrote the following dismal description:[42]

We have never had a change of diet, which you know is con-

[37] R. B. Elliott to R. K. Scott, September 13, 1869, South Carolina Military Affairs file.

[38] *Annual Report of the Adjutant General of the State of Louisiana, 1874*, p. 18.

[39] General Order 7, April 18, 1874, AGO files, state of Tennessee.

[40] Clayton, *Aftermath in Arkansas*, p. 133.

[41] R. B. Elliott to R. K. Scott, September 13, 1869, South Carolina Military Affairs file.

[42] Quoted in Patton, *Reconstruction in Tennessee*, p. 198.

trary to the laws of nature, hygiene, and army regulations. We draw meal, bacon, sugar and coffee and occasionally a small quantity of beans, salt and soup, all of which is deficient in quantity and inferior in quality, which we have to carry daily for one mile for lack of water.

Shortages of equipment were further causes for discontent. Requests for arms and ammunition were continually forwarded to headquarters by field commanders, many of whom were forced to arm their men as best they could.[43] Although lack of arms was a serious matter, it was not nearly so destructive of morale as the shortage of uniforms. One officer reported that many of his men "had not sufficient clothing to protect them in ordinary weather, much less when exposed. . . ."[44] On Christmas night of 1868, a detachment of Arkansas militia encamped in the woods near Madison were blanketed by a six-inch snowfall,[45] and because there were no heavy uniforms there was much suffering among the men. The captain of a Negro unit in Tennessee wrote this pitiful account of his men: "They are laying on the ground at night in the dew. I want blankets, coats, tents, drawers, and shirts. The men are to go on a march in one or two days and have not the things to go with."[46]

Medical attention, when furnished at all, was casual and restricted. For example, General Cooper instructed commanding officers of Tennessee State Guards units that in cases of "sickness due to misconduct" (the military euphemism for venereal disease) physicians were to medi-

---

[43] Clayton, *Aftermath in Arkansas*, p. 126.

[44] Colonel —. —. Watson to P. Clayton, October 3, 1889, quoted in *ibid.*

[45] *Ibid.*

[46] Quoted in Patton, *Reconstruction in Tennessee*, p. 199.

cate not at the expense of the state but at the personal expense of the persons so afflicted.[47]

One last factor tending to cool enthusiasm for militia duty was the omnipresent evidence of Conservative enmity. Whenever a militia unit made an appearance, the soldiers were jeered at, taunted, and insulted. The Tennessee militiamen, for example, were called "damned cowardly Brownlow sons of b——s"[48] and were informed that their detractors had no earthly use "for any . . . Brownlow militia, socially, politically or any other way."[49] By encouraging militiamen to desert, Conservatives deliberately undermined the effectiveness of the organization. Outright assaults were repeatedly made on Negro troops. Sniping, ambushes, and midnight raids on bivouacked detachments were fairly common, and on one occasion the citizens of Rogersville, Tennessee, engaged in a rock-throwing war with a militia company.[50] The constant threat of attack was responsible for the fact that many militiamen "slept on their arms at night."[51]

Of course, many of the defects, shortcomings, problems, and afflictions of the militia movement were "institutional"; they have existed in one form or another in almost all volunteer organizations of citizen-soldiers. They were greatly intensified in the Reconstruction militia, however, and it is not surprising that the movement was militarily ineffective. Led by officers who were indifferent, ineffi-

[47] General Order 7, August 9, 1867, General Order Book, Tennessee State Guards, 1867, AGO files, state of Tennessee.

[48] Captain —. —. Hall to General Joseph Cooper, November 24, 1867, AGO files, state of Tennessee.

[49] Captain —. —. Clingan to General Joseph Cooper, July 11, 1867, AGO files, state of Tennessee.

[50] Anonymous letter to J. P. Brownlow, August 24, 1867, AGO files, state of Tennessee.

[51] *New York Herald*, July 24, 1870.

cient, and, more often than not, incompetent; neglected by the politicians in whose interests they were fighting; and living oftentimes under frightful hardships in the midst of an implacable enemy, the fact that they survived for any length of time stands as a tribute to pertinacity and devotion to a cause.

VIII. The Conservative Reaction

FROM ITS VERY INCEPTION, the Negro militia experiment was bitterly opposed by Southern white Conservatives. Throughout the entire period and at every stage of development they continued their attack on the movement. Militia laws were challenged in state legislatures, where they were condemned as sinister political maneuvers. When, after passage of these laws, attempts were made to arm and organize troops, denouncements by Conservatives grew more shrill, for they professed to see in this action "a dangerous offensive design" to spy on them.[1] When militia units were actually put to use, the outcry of the opposition became deafening, and the troops were charged with every conceivable crime. The Conservative-controlled press was the most popular medium for the transmission of this propaganda, and editorial pages were filled with harsh language against the opposition. Not only were local Negroes, carpetbaggers, and scalawags excoriated, but even the inhabitants of the North received their share of abuse. Perhaps the height of vituperation was reached in an anti-Yankee rhyme that appeared in the *Panola* (Mississippi) *Star*. After a savage and almost hysterical attack on Northerners in general, the poet requested that Southerners be remembered as a people[2]

> What hates the Cotton Mather
> And the Roger Williams stock,
> That dirty pile of Hell's manure
> First dumped on Plymouth's Rock.

Opposition to the militia was not confined to verbal as-

[1] W. W. Davis, *Civil War and Reconstruction in Florida*, p. 544. (Hereafter cited as *Reconstruction in Florida*.)
[2] Quoted in S. Misc. Doc. 45, 44th Cong., 2d Sess., p. 1002.

sault. As the Democratic party in the South regained its strength, other and bolder measures were adopted in an effort to neutralize militia effectiveness. Although the actual destruction of these forces was to come later by means of armed military counterforces, efficient operation was seriously impaired by a miscellany of Conservative tactics that included the use of legal stratagems, threats, bribes, seizures of equipment destined for the militia, and direct retaliation upon militiamen.

Within the general category of opposition through political strategy, the Conservatives employed several techniques. Prominent Democrats led the fight in state legislatures against passage of militia laws and further attempted to block enabling acts.[3] When unable to defeat these appropriations outright, they resorted to use of the injunction to prevent expenditure of funds. The North Carolina treasurer was specifically forbidden to pay militia troops out of the military appropriation,[4] while in Louisiana money that had been set aside for the purchase of uniforms was enjoined by the attorney general.[5] Mississippi Democrats secured an injunction to restrain the state auditor from issuing warrants against militia appropriations.[6]

Impeachment was another legal weapon used by the Conservatives, primarily against Radical governors under

[3] Militia laws apparently figured consistently among campaign issues. In Louisiana, for example, one group threatened not to vote for any man unless he would refuse to support militia appropriations. (Lonn, *Reconstruction in Louisiana*, p. 67.) A Mississippi political club adopted a resolution advocating "the appropriation of nothing" in support of the militia. (Garner, *Reconstruction in Mississippi*, p. 297.)

[4] Hamilton, *Reconstruction in North Carolina*, p. 531.

[5] *Annual Report of the Adjutant General of the State of Louisiana, 1874*, p. 7.

[6] S. Rep. 527, 44th Cong., 1st Sess., p. 6. Garner, *Reconstruction in Mississippi*, p. 384.

whose direction militia forces had been organized. Threats of impeachment were continually heard, and abortive attempts in that direction were made against Governor Clayton, in Arkansas, and Governor Warmoth, in Louisiana. Governor Ames, of Mississippi, was impeached but resigned his office after a compromise that included the withdrawal of official charges against him (see Chapter VI). North Carolinians impeached Governor Holden, and one of the charges against him was "unlawfully recruiting a large body of troops. . . ."[7] Before the trial, Holden "got religion," was converted and publicly baptized,[8] an act that led one editor to remark that "no record of any similar preparation for impeachment" could be discovered but that its effect would be "watched by jurists with deep interests."[9] In spite of his reformation, he was convicted, removed from office, and disqualified for future office-holding in that state.[10] The fact that several Republicans voted for his conviction led one Negro legislator to comment that the Governor had been "bit by his own dogs."[11]

Still another technique for legally sabotaging the militia was the support of laws specifically designed to lower military efficiency or to make soldiering a less attractive avocation. Outright disbandment was accomplished in Tennessee,[12] and in Texas the active-duty troops were transferred to the reserve militia.[13] Existing laws were either repealed or modified wherever possible. In Mississippi, for

---

[7] Archibald Henderson, *North Carolina, the Old State and the New,* Vol. II, p. 332. (Hereafter cited as *North Carolina.*)

[8] Hamilton, *Reconstruction in North Carolina,* p. 545.

[9] *The Nation,* December 22, 1870, quoted in *ibid.*

[10] Henderson, *North Carolina,* Vol. II, p. 332.

[11] Hamilton, *Reconstruction in North Carolina,* p. 543.

[12] J. A. Sharp, "The Downfall of the Radicals in Tennessee," *The East Tennessee Historical Society's Publications,* No. 5 (1933), p. 108.

[13] Ramsdell, *Reconstruction in Texas,* p. 313.

example, the pay of officers was cut to five cents a day,[14] making service considerably less rewarding. Adjutant generals were treated rather spitefully in that their salaries were frequently cut to practically nothing.[15] The Texas legislators amended the law of that state so as to deprive the governor of exclusive control of the forces,[16] and in Louisiana laws granting preferential treatment or exemptions to militiamen were repealed.[17] Whenever Negro legislators could be persuaded to support these maneuvers, they were lionized by their Conservative colleagues; a Mississippi Negro who voted against the Ames-sponsored police bill was publicly presented with a gold-headed cane.[18]

In addition to such legal attacks, Conservatives displayed their hostility to the militia by employing several other measures short of actual force. The verbal onslaught continued unabated. Militia units were subjected to a continuing program of sarcastic abuse. Newspapers printed such taunting queries as: "Why do not the white Radicals volunteer in the colored militia? They are just as good as the colored men."[19] When a rumor of Brownlow's death was circulated in Tennessee, a group of Conservatives called upon one of his supporters, a fuel merchant, and inquired about the price of 1,100 cords of wood they wanted to purchase in order "to make hell hotter for him."[20] The North Carolina State Militia, whose initials

[14] Garner, *Reconstruction in Mississippi*, p. 411.

[15] *Proceedings of the Tax-Payer's Convention of South Carolina, 1871*, p. 107; Hamilton, *Reconstruction in North Carolina*, p. 559.

[16] Ramsdell, *Reconstruction in Texas*, p. 313.

[17] *Annual Report of the Adjutant General of the State of Louisiana, 1874*, p. 11.

[18] Garner, *Reconstruction in Mississippi*, p. 328.

[19] *Hinds County* (Miss.) *Gazette*, October 13, 1875.

[20] *Report of Evidence Taken before the Military Committee, 35th General Assembly, State of Tennessee, 1868*, p. 34.

N.C.S.M. appeared in their insignia, were derisively called the "Negro, Carpetbag, Scalawag Militia."[21]

Acts of a more threatening nature designed to intimidate Negroes were frequently perpetrated. In Mississippi, for instance, a group of whites descended upon the town of Clinton and took down names of Negroes, implying that retribution would soon be visited upon them.[22] Negro leaders were ostentatiously enrolled in "Dead Books,"[23] and coffins were paraded through the streets marked with the names of prominent Radicals and labeled with such inspriptions as "Dead, damned and delivered."[24] One of the most effective methods used by the Conservatives to intimidate the militia was the firing of cannon. These guns were very much in demand not only for their persuasive power but also for use should warfare actually break out. A leader of the Mississippi Democrats borrowed a cannon from Governor Warmoth, of Louisiana, during the honeymoon period of co-operation on the Greeley candidacy. He assured Warmoth, of course, that Mississippi Liberals and Democrats were working in "perfect accord."[25] During the campaign of 1875, Mississippi Democrats, using what apparently must have been great powers of persuasion, borrowed a cannon from the commander of United States troops stationed in Jackson. During a subsequent parade that passed in front of the governor's mansion, the gun was deliberately fired near enough to the building to break

---

[21] Hamilton, *Reconstruction in North Carolina*, p. 347.

[22] Anonymous letter to Adelbert Ames, September 6, 1875, Ames Papers.

[23] Wharton, *The Negro in Mississippi*, p. 188.

[24] Testimony of John Ellis, H.R. Rep. 2, 43d Cong., 2d Sess., pp. 343–44; S. Rep. 527, 44th Cong., 1st Sess., p. 279.

[25] H. Barksdale to Henry Clay Warmoth, August 5, 1872, Warmoth Papers.

several windows. Although no action was taken against the paraders, the federal commander was court-martialed for allowing his ordnance to be used in so irregular a manner.[26] There can be little doubt that terrorization through cannonading was effective. A Negro militiaman involved in the South Carolina troubles testified that when the cannon procured by the whites in his neighborhood was first fired he cried out to his brothers-in-arms: "Jesus! God! We are all done killed!"[27]

Disarming Negroes was another practice aimed at destroying their military effectiveness. Individual militiamen were sometimes attacked for this purpose, and in one section of Mississippi even their pocketknives were taken away from them.[28] Governors experienced increasing difficulties in supplying their forces with enough material to keep them in a state of combat readiness. Owing to the persistent spying of whites, successful delivery depended upon acting in the utmost secrecy, and failure to exercise sufficient caution inevitably led to losses of equipment. Governor Clayton, of Arkansas, suffered one such bitter experience while attempting to procure arms for his militia in 1868. An agent whom he had sent to Detroit purchased 4,000 rifles, 400,000 rounds of cartridges, 1½ million percussion caps, and a large quantity of gunpowder.[29] These materials were shipped via railroad as far south as Memphis, where they were to be picked up and transported by steamer to Little Rock for the avowed purpose

[26] Garner, *Reconstruction in Mississippi*, p. 374.
[27] Testimony of Harry Mays, S. Misc. Doc. 48, Vol. I, 44th Cong., 2d Sess., p. 32.
[28] Deposition of Sheriff John P. Matthews of Copiah County, Mississippi, September 13, 1875, Ames Papers.
[29] Fletcher, *Arkansas*, p. 218.

of "preserving the peace on election day and [of] securing a free ballot to all."[30] When no steamboat captain in
Memphis would agree to take the cargo aboard, the re-
sourceful Clayton chartered a steamboat, the *Hesper*,
which was lying alongside the wharf at Little Rock, and
sent it to Memphis to pick up the equipment. On October
15, 1868, the *Hesper* set sail from Memphis with its valuable cargo stowed safely in the hold.[31] While taking on
wood some 20 miles downriver from the city, the *Hesper*
was suddenly challenged by a steam tug, the *Nettie Jones*,
which was carrying approximately fifty armed and masked
men. The tug maneuvered alongside the *Hesper*, and
the masked men boarded the steamer, overpowered the
crew, and dumped the entire consignment of costly arms
and ammunition into the muddy waters of the Mississippi
River.[32]

Governor Reed suffered a similar misfortune in his attempts to arm the Florida Militia. After having purchased
2,000 rifles in the North, he had them shipped to Tallahassee by train. On the night of November 6, 1868, the train
carrying the arms was held up between Lake City and
Madison, en route to the capital; the guns were thrown
from the train and those not deliberately broken were
spirited away.[33]

In South Carolina, an amphibious operation by a hand-
ful of white volunteers resulted in a sensational seizure
of arms destined for delivery to the Negro militia. Two
thousand Enfield rifles smuggled into the state from Wash-

[30] *New York Daily Tribune*, November 4, 1868.

[31] Fletcher, *Arkansas*, p. 219.

[32] Clayton, *Aftermath in Arkansas*, p. 108; Fletcher, *Arkansas*, p.
219; *New York Daily Tribune*, November 4, 1868.

[33] *New York Times*, November 7, 1868, cited in Davis, *Reconstruction in Florida*, p. 567.

ington were temporarily deposited in the Savannah depot awaiting distribution. Twelve volunteers from a Charleston rifle company sailed to Savannah aboard two pleasure yachts, the *Eleanor* and the *Flirt,* overpowered the guards and stole the guns.[34]

Confiscation of arms belonging to militia units was not uncommon. On several occasions, whites persuaded militiamen to turn in their guns to some central depository as a move toward keeping the peace. No sooner was this done than the whites would unlawfully enter the storage place and seize the arms.[35] Quite often the same guns would be distributed among members of white rifle clubs.[36]

Such actions by Conservatives caused considerable concern among supporters of the Radical regimes. Governors were constantly being warned to beware of enemy intentions and to exercise great caution in shipping arms into the countryside.[37] In order to distribute arms successfully, governors were forced to resort to subterfuge. One consignment of rifles was shipped into Newberry, South Carolina, marked as "agricultural implements."[38] In Arkansas, 2,000 Springfield rifles were imported as *Arkansas State Reports,* and 13,000 rounds of ammunition escaped detection only because the shipper had wisely labeled the cases "whisky."[39]

In addition to legal stratagems, intimidation, and seizure of arms, the Conservatives also employed the technique of personal retaliation against militiamen and their

[34] Alfred B. Williams, *Hampton and His Red Shirts,* p. 225.
[35] S. Misc. Doc. 48, Vol. I, 44th Cong., 2d Sess., p. 857; Simkins, *Pitchfork Ben Tillman,* p. 61.
[36] S. Rep. 527, 44th Cong., 1st Sess., p. 97.
[37] S. W. Gere to Adelbert Ames, October 15, 1875, Ames Papers.
[38] *Columbia* (S.C.) *Daily Register,* August 15, 1876.
[39] Johnson, "The Brooks-Baxter War," 122–74.

leaders by means of social ostracism, economic discrimination, and physical violence.

The most famous case of social ostracism involved General James Longstreet, who, after allying himself with Republican politicians in Louisiana, assumed active command of the Negro militia (see Chapter V). His political pronouncements in favor of Republican principles gave rise to some opposition from erstwhile friends, but his appearance as commander of the Negro forces in New Orleans was considered unforgivable and led to bitter, even vituperative, attacks upon him. He was virtually eliminated from accepted social circles in that city and was pointedly ignored in public by persons whom he had known well.[40]

Economic sanctions were also levied against militiamen as a feature of the retaliatory program inaugurated by the Conservatives. Landlords pledged themselves neither to rent land nor to give employment to Negro militiamen, and the vow was rigidly adhered to since social ostracism was the reward of the apostate.[41] This tactic was quite effective. Paris Simkins, Negro legislator from Edgefield, introduced a resolution designed to protect South Carolina militiamen from being discharged and driven away from farms where they were employed.[42] George W. Kirk, who commanded the North Carolina forces, regretfully reported to Governor Holden on one occasion that "the farmers and others in Caswell [County] are turning off their hands and refusing to pay them their wages."[43]

[40] Eckenrode and Conrad, *James Longstreet*, pp. 372–75.
[41] Simkins, *Pitchfork Ben Tillman*, p. 60.
[42] Reynolds, *Reconstruction in South Carolina*, p. 305.
[43] George W. Kirk to William W. Holden, August 3, 1870, Holden Papers.

Personal violence was visited not only upon Negro militiamen but also upon whites associated with the militia movement. T. M. Shoffner, author of the North Carolina militia act that bore his name, learned of a plot against his life in 1870. Word was spread that the Orange County Ku Klux Klan had voted his death and intended to ship his body as a gift to Governor Holden. Whether or not the rumor had any real foundation, Shoffner was so thoroughly alarmed that he removed himself to the more tranquil state of Indiana.[44] When Holden finally armed his troops, he put them under the command of George W. Kirk, of Tennessee, with a New Jerseyite named Bergen as his assistant. After the Kirk-Holden War had run its course, both the Governor's henchmen landed in jail. Holden visited Kirk during his incarceration and helped him escape from the state by making him a gift of $140, which enabled him to get to the fittingly named town of Freedom, Tennessee,[45] the first stop on a journey to Washington, where he soon joined the police force guarding the federal buildings. Bergen also managed to escape from the state, after having once been run down by bloodhounds.[46] He too subsequently turned up in Washington, where Grant nominated him for the consulship at Pernambuco. The nomination was not confirmed, and Grant withdrew it, presumably with the concurrence of Governor Holden.[47] Bergen later remarked with noticeable bitterness that in reward for his services he received "94 days imprisonment and six weeks pay."[48]

Compared to Joseph Crews, of South Carolina, these

[44] Hamilton, *Reconstruction in North Carolina*, p. 470.
[45] Holden, *Memoirs*, p. 92.
[46] Hamilton, *Reconstruction in North Carolina*, pp. 532–33.
[47] Holden, *Memoirs*, p. 91.
[48] S. Rep. 1, 42d Cong., 1st Sess., p. 152.

two men were extremely fortunate. Crews was the moving spirit behind the organization of a Negro militia troop in Laurens during the administration of Governor Scott. After organizing the unit, he assumed active command and in so doing became a target for the bitter hatred of the local Conservatives. As early as 1870, he and his followers were involved in a fight with local whites in which one Negro was killed and two others were wounded. Crews eluded the vengeful whites by hiding out in a hollow log and later fleeing on a railroad handcar, hidden under a piece of canvass and disguised as a quarter of beef. When conditions in Laurens settled down, he returned and took up his career again and remained there until late in the summer of 1875, when, while riding along in his buggy some four miles outside town, he was ambushed and fatally wounded by a shotgun blast.[49] The *New York Herald* reported that the "Honorable Joe Crews, republican politician of note" was dying of buckshot wounds and that the Governor of South Carolina had put a price on the head of his attacker.[50] Another notorious crime was the murder in North Carolina of one Colonel Sheppard, a former Union Army man from Pennsylvania who had organized the Negro militia in Jones County.[51]

Retaliatory attacks on whites were few in number in comparison to actions taken against Negro militiamen. The latter were subjected to every imaginable species of intimidation and violence.[52] Threats were hurled at them constantly and often at persons only remotely connected with the militia. An Arkansas horse-dealer named Mc-

[49] Leland, *A Voice from South Carolina*, pp. 52–67, 134.
[50] *New York Herald*, September 9, 1875.
[51] Testimony of R. T. Bosher, S. Rep. 1, 42d Cong., 1st Sess., p. 102.
[52] Simkins and Woody, *South Carolina during Reconstruction*, p. 444.

Creary was threatened with hanging for selling horses to the militia,[53] and an aged Negro in Tennessee was visited by a masked deputation and threatened severely because his son was engaged in raising a militia company.[54]

Raids on the homes of militiamen for the purpose of destroying their personal property occurred frequently. A South Carolina militia captain described how he had watched marauders "taking down my pictures and breaking up my furniture. They broke up everything I had in the world; they took all my clothes, my mattress, my feather bed, cut it in pieces and scattered it everywhere...."[55]

Negro militia captains were singled out and executed. Captain A. J. Haynes, for example, was murdered on the streets of Marion, Arkansas, in broad daylight. Haynes was commander of the local militia detachment and had for some time been on "unfriendly terms" with Clarence Collier, an alleged member of the local Ku Klux Klan who at the age of twenty-one already had one notch in his gun handle. On July 15, 1869, when Haynes was walking along the main street of town, Collier approached him and without warning emptied both loads of a double-barreled shotgun into his body. To make sure Haynes was dead, Collier fired five revolver shots into the fallen body, strolled back into a nearby store where he had left his coat, put it on, came back outside, and rode away from town unmolested.[56]

An even more brutal murder was that of Charles Cald-

[53] Clayton, *Aftermath in Arkansas*, p. 101.

[54] *Report of Evidence Taken before the Military Committee, 35th General Assembly, State of Tennessee, 1868*, p. 54.

[55] Testimony of Doc Adams, S. Misc. Doc. 48, Vol. I, 44th Cong., 2d Sess., p. 43.

[56] Clayton, *Aftermath in Arkansas*, pp. 175–86.

well, the fiery mulatto state senator of Mississippi. Caldwell had been placed in command of the Negro troops
mobilized by Governor Ames after the Clinton riot on
September 4, 1875. While serving in this capacity, he
led an expedition that left Jackson in October, 1875, carrying arms for distribution to the militia at Edwards Station.[57] Although his forces were not attacked en route, the
trip caused much excitement, and Caldwell became a
marked man. Two months later, during the Christmas
holidays, his enemies struck. One of the whites living in
Clinton invited Caldwell down into the cellar of a local
building under the guise of sharing a companionable drink
in honor of the season. The unsuspecting Caldwell accepted, and the two men disappeared down the stairway.
When the drinks had been poured, a toast was proposed.
The clinking of the glasses was the prearranged signal for
a strategically placed killer who held Caldwell in his gun-
sight. As the glasses touched, a rifle report shattered the
quiet, and Caldwell fell bleeding to the cellar floor. The
wounded Negro, displaying great courage, refused to beg
for his life but only entreated them to take him out of the
cellar so that he might die in the open air. A local preacher
carried him out into the street, where the conspirators
gathered to finish their job. Caldwell's last statement to
them was a calm instruction to remember that they had
killed a brave man, not a coward. His body was ripped by
a volley, and his corpse was grotesquely turned complete-
ly over by the impact of innumerable shots fired at close
range.[58]

A similar case was that of Jim Williams, in South

[57] *Jackson* (Miss.) *Weekly Clarion,* October 20, 1875.
[58] This story has been reconstructed from the testimony of Mrs.
Charles Caldwell, S. Rep. 527, 44th Cong., 1st Sess., 435–40.

Carolina. Williams was the leader of a Negro militia unit in lower York County. His aggressive leadership caused the whites to demand disbandment of his company.[59] Williams' refusal to comply was his death warrant. Early on the morning of March 7, 1871, his lifeless body was found hanging in the public square with a large placard pinned to it bearing the inscription: "Jim Williams gone to his last muster."[60] A curious sidelight to this affair was that it involved the United States government in an international incident. A York County physician, Dr. J. Rufus Bratton, who had been implicated in the Williams murder, fled the country and settled down in London, Ontario, to practice. One night during the summer of 1872, he was seized, gagged, blindfolded, and taken across the border, where he was turned over to two United States marshals for return to South Carolina. Canadian authorities made insistent demands for his immediate release. After a slight delay, Bratton was freed and returned to Canada, there to remain until 1876, when he returned to York County to live. No legal action was taken against him for the Williams murder.[61]

The catalogue of crimes could be continued indefinitely. Equally bloody are the stories of how James Rainey, a South Carolina militia captain, was taken from his home and hanged, or how Alexander Leech was shot and his body thrown in a nearby creek.[62] Other militiamen too numerous to give individual accounts of were slaughtered in similar orgies of violence.

[59] Reynolds, *Reconstruction in South Carolina*, p. 188.
[60] Louis F. Post, "A Carpetbagger in South Carolina," *Journal of Negro History*, Vol. X (1925), p. 61.
[61] For details of the Bratton case, see Reynolds, *Reconstruction in South Carolina*, p. 201.
[62] H.R. Rep. 22, Vol. III, Part 3, 42d Cong., 2d Sess., p. 1472.

Yet the measures described in this chapter did not really destroy the Negro militia. The legal stratagems, threats, and confiscations were merely tokens of the white man's resentment, and even his acts of violence against militiamen were sporadic in nature. They undermined the effectiveness of the militia movement, to be sure; but actual destruction was to come only after the full force of the white man's fury was channeled into the organization of armed military counterforces within the Southern states.

IX. Nemesis

ALTHOUGH OPPOSITION to the Negro militia was manifested in various ways from the very beginning of the
movement, the final devastating blow was the organization by its opponents of armed military counterforces in
the Southern states. Where earlier forms of reaction had
been limited either to measures short of force or to isolated attacks on individual militiamen, the new volunteer
rifle companies were specifically designed as instruments
of mass force to overwhelm and smash not only the Negro
battalions themselves but also the political regimes that
employed them. Such extreme measures were not needed
in all states, for in several places the Democratic party
had returned to power by other means. In the few remaining states where the Radicals tenaciously maintained
their hold, Conservative leaders became more and more partial to the sentiment that victory could be accomplished
"in only one way, BY ARMED FORCE."[1] Hence, during
the latter years of Reconstruction, armed military companies were organized and played increasingly important
roles in overturning Radical regimes in several states, particularly in Louisiana, Mississippi, and South Carolina.
This politico-military movement was known by such
varied titles as White Line, White League, People's Club,
Red Shirts, and White Man's Party.

A great deal of misinformation exists about the White
Line movement, largely because of the misrepresentations
sponsored by both Radicals and Conservatives. On one
hand, Radicals claimed that the movement was merely a

[1] *Charleston* (S.C.) *News and Courier*, May 8, 1876, quoted in W.
Allen, *Governor Chamberlain's Administration in South Carolina*, p.
275.

revival of the Ku Klux Klan. One governor, in a letter to a friend, stated that "the old rebel forces are being reorganized not under the name of the Ku Klux but as the White Leagues, with the same ultimate object in view as had by the Ku Klux."[2] Actually, there appears to have been no direct connection between the Klan and the White League, though their programs did reflect similarities. Both had missions that centered about the doctrine of white supremacy. Both unhesitatingly turned to the use of force and violence whenever necessary to attain their goals. However, the similarity goes no deeper. The White Line had a narrower, more specific aim than that of the Klan. It was primarily concerned with the political problem of restoring Conservative rule, usually in one particular election, by a carefully prepared program of fraud, violence, and intimidation. In addition to the concentrated nature of its mission, the White Line also differed from the Klan in that it was not fundamentally a secret organization. Clandestine meetings and exotic ritual found no place in the movement. So open were their activities that in most localities the names of members and even of the leaders were common knowledge. The lack of emphasis upon secrecy undoubtedly stemmed from a growing conviction that interference by the national government was becoming less and less likely.

The Conservative legend of the White Line movement has also contributed to the continuing misinterpretations. In order to furnish justification for the excesses that were committed, the defensive and protective roles of the clubs were played up. As painted in Conservative whitewash, the movement was portrayed solely as a means of defending the white race. Newspapers printed editorials claim-

2 Adelbert Ames to F. C. Harris, August 4, 1874, Ames Papers.

ing that as long as white military companies existed "the good people . . . will have protectors and rallying points,"[3] and Conservative leaders repeated over and over again that they had organized "purely for protection; not for any political purpose in the world, but to protect ourselves against the encroachments of the blacks."[4] One overly sympathetic observer even reported that the league members "held no meetings, named no committees, elected no chiefs. It was a sentiment rather than a society."[5]

Such partisan views of the movement generally either overstated or understated the case. Actually, the White Line was something distinct and set apart from the Ku Klux Klan, and its mission was by no means confined to defensive or protective measures. It was an aggressive political instrument welded into a military mold for a definite purpose. It was, indeed, considerably more than a mere sentiment; it was carefully organized, and its activities were planned in minute detail and executed by chosen leaders. Perhaps the most effective way to correct the erroneous or only half-true impressions that have persisted is to examine the movement in the light of available evidence and report what it really was as opposed to what it was popularly claimed to be.

To grasp the significance of the White Line movement, one must realize from the beginning that it was essentially of a political nature. It is not too great a generalization to say that the rifle companies were merely the armed wing of the Democratic party. In Mississippi, these companies were under the control of General J. Z. George, who as campaign manager of the state Democratic party

[3] *Hinds County* (Miss.) *Gazette*, September 22, 1875.
[4] S. Rep. 527, 44th Cong., 1st Sess., p. lxvii.
[5] Dixon, *White Conquest*, Vol. II, p. 24.

Thomas Nast's characterization of the White League move-ment in the South (Harper's Weekly, *1874*)

masterminded its political strategy. In South Carolina, the role of the rifle companies was stated explicitly in no less conspicuous a place than the campaign plan of the Democratic party.[6] Nor was it a mere coincidence that in mid-September, 1874, when the Democrats in Louisiana fought a pitched battle against the Radicals for control of the Statehouse, the "militia" championing the Conservative cause was almost exclusively composed of members of the New Orleans White League.[7]

Although essentially political in nature and in aims, leagues were deliberately organized into military formations and trained in the use of force. The types of formations varied, although most of them were either infantry or cavalry units designated respectively as rifle companies and sabre clubs. Most clubs possessed at least one piece of artillery and in many instances owned several field pieces. Each club had a full complement of officers, many of whom were experienced soldiers.[8] The military features of the organization were clearly described in the instructions circulated in South Carolina:[9]

The Democratic military clubs are to be armed with rifles and pistols and such other arms as they may command. They are to be divided into two companies, one of the old men, the other of the young; an experienced captain or commander to be

[6] The South Carolina campaign of 1876 was closely patterned after the Mississippi, or "Shotgun," plan and was drawn up by Martin W. Gary. A copy of this detailed strategy can be found in the appendix of Simkins and Woody, *South Carolina during Reconstruction*, pp. 564–69.

[7] *New York Herald*, September 15, 1874.

[8] J. Z. George, of Mississippi; M. C. Butler, of South Carolina; and Frederick N. Ogden, of Louisiana, were all former high-ranking Confederate officers.

[9] M. W. Gary's plan for the South Carolina campaign of 1876, quoted in Simkins and Woody, *South Carolina during Reconstruction*, pp. 564–69.

placed over each. . . . Each company is to have a first and second lieutenant. . . . The number of ten privates is to be the unit of organization.

In addition to the fact that the clubs were political in nature and military in organization, they had a definite purpose that went considerably beyond the mere function of protection. Since their real mission did not lend itself to publicity, Conservative leaders turned to the use of guile and subterfuge when explaining the reasons for their existence. Typical of such tactics was the following letter to the Governor of South Carolina:[10]

Dear Sir:

At the solicitation of several others I write to ask your permission to organize a Sabre Club, for our own amusement, in Norris Township, Edgefield County.

Various other arguments, equally misleading, were advanced in justification of maintaining armed rifle companies. It was often claimed, for example, that the purpose was "chiefly social."[11] One member described his particular club as a "social organization" designed to cultivate the virtues of friendship and manly exercise,"[12] while another made the claim that the only purpose of the White League in his area was "for our amusement and to improve the horsemanship of the young men of this vicinity."[13] In spite of these protestations, the move-

[10] J. Boatwright to Franklin J. Moses, Jr., August 6, 1874, Franklin J. Moses, Jr., Papers.

[11] R. S. Beckman to Daniel H. Chamberlain, June 24, 1874, South Carolina Military Affairs file.

[12] R. R. Hemphill to Daniel H. Chamberlain, June 13, 1875, South Carolina Military Affairs file.

[13] R. L. Craft to Daniel H. Chamberlain, June 16, 1876, South Carolina Military Affairs file.

ment did have a definite aim that concisely stated by the editor of the *Opelousas* (Louisiana) *Courier:* "The object of the White League is to put the control of the state government into the hands of the white people of the state."[14]

Participation in the movement was not restricted to those of voting age. Boys over sixteen were included on the list of eligibles in South Carolina,[15] and there is one case on record where a rifle company was formed by boys "between the ages of six and ten years."[16] White women were very active not only in recruiting for the volunteer companies[17] but also in furnishing them with military insignia and trappings. The Abbeville, South Carolina, club, for example, was presented with a flag by Miss Kate Parker.[18]

Meetings were held periodically, sometimes to deal with political affairs and at other times merely to go through their drills "according to Upton's Tactics."[19] Meetings were called by means of a prearranged system of signals that made it possible for a company to be mustered within a couple of hours.[20] Normally, a cannon shot was the agreed signal, but when such equipment was not available league members improvised in the following manner: "They took a couple of anvils and put them together, one on top of the other, and filled the hole with powder and fired them off whenever they wanted to call

[14] Issue dated, July 4, 1874, quoted in Brewster, *Sketches,* p. 175.
[15] Simkins and Woody, *South Carolina during Reconstruction,* pp. 564–69.
[16] S. Misc. Doc. 48, Vol. III, 44th Cong., 2d Sess., p. 624.
[17] Morgan, *Yazoo,* p. 455.
[18] S. Misc. Doc. 48, Vol. III, 44th Cong., 2d Sess., p. 624.
[19] *Ibid.,* p. 109.
[20] Simkins, *Pitchfork Ben Tillman,* p. 58.

the club together. It made a noise very much like a cannon, and can be heard eight or ten miles."[21]

The extent and number of military companies is difficult to determine accurately, but as a generalization it can be said that they appeared in almost every county where Republicans were either in the majority or actually in control of public offices. Governor Chamberlain estimated that there were at least 290 rifle clubs in South Carolina at one time;[22] a source in Mississippi stated that nearly one-half of the white population of voting age in that state was enrolled in the movement.[23]

Military units thus organized were well armed. Radical governors received many letters similar to this one describing White Line activities:[24]

Dear Govnor: We here give you notice that the white people of this towrne have jest receved, by express from New Orleans, three boxes of guns and also some boxse of pistols for the porpus of a riot in this place, whils we have not got a gun or do not want any disturbemenst. . . .

Such reports were not exaggerated, for arms were plentiful among leaguers. The 2,000 members of the New Orleans League furnish an interesting illustration. Two-thirds of them were armed with Belgian muskets purchased in New York, almost all of them had pistols, and the club also possessed two cannon.[25] One outfit in Mississippi had cavalry, infantry, and artillery units well equipped with shotguns, needle guns, and 6-pound can-

[21] S. Rep. 527, 44th Cong., 1st Sess., p. 88.
[22] S. Misc. Doc. 48, 44th Cong., 2d Sess., p. 509.
[23] S. Rep. 527, 44th Cong., 1st Sess., p. xxv.
[24] W. K. Jones to Adelbert Ames, September 10, 1875, quoted in S. Rep. 527, 44th Cong., 1st Sess., p. 19.
[25] Brewster, *Sketches*, p. 172.

non loaded with scrap iron.[26] A. T. Morgan, Yazoo City's leading Radical, described that city's military organization as he observed it from a place of hiding following the riot of September 1, 1875: "They were as well armed and under as perfect discipline, apparently, as any troops in our late armies were. Including the cavalry company from the county, there were not less than three hundred armed white men in the town. Their weapons were Winchester rifles, needle guns, double-barrel shotguns and pistols."[27]

Several methods were employed to secure necessary arms for the rifle companies. So successful were these measures that Democratic spokesmen were able to boast publicly that the clubs were "fully armed, equipped and drilled."[28] Most of these arms were obtained by purchase, and funds were raised in various ways. Although there is no actual proof of the charge that money was contributed by the national Democratic organization, there is considerable evidence that funds were privately subscribed in the North.[29] Local subscriptions also paid for a share of the arms. Older men who were not expected to bear arms were requested to outfit younger men. In South Carolina, each rifle-company captain was instructed[30]

to see that his men are well armed and provided with at least thirty rounds of ammunition. The captain of the young men is to provide a Baggage wagon, in which three days rations for

[26] John Meek to Adelbert Ames, November 2, 1875, Ames Papers.
[27] Morgan, *Yazoo*, p. 474.
[28] Wharton, *The Negro in Mississippi*, p. 187.
[29] John R. Lynch, *Facts of Reconstruction*, p. 141; Walter L. Fleming, *Civil War and Reconstruction in Alabama*, p. 791.
[30] Martin W. Gary's plan for the South Carolina campaign of 1876. Quoted in Simkins and Woody, *South Carolina during Reconstruction*, pp. 564–69.

the horses and three days rations for the men are to be stored . . . in order that they may be prepared at a moments notice to move to any point in the county when ordered by the chairman of the executive committee.

Still another method of obtaining guns was to steal them from Negro militia units. Because this happened so frequently, Radical governors were constantly being warned to use every precaution when shipping arms. In spite of all such action, seizures were fairly common. In Mississippi, for example, guns stolen from militiamen were later seen in use by White Liners as they drilled.[31] Similar cases that occurred in South Carolina have been described in Chapter VIII. Seizures and thefts apparently assumed sizable proportions, for one adjutant general officially proclaimed as potentially dangerous the fact that "a large number of the arms of the state are in the hands of independent organizations . . . not under the control of the law that governs the militia."[32]

Since the political objective of the White Liners was achieved in due time, it is interesting to note the tactics they employed to achieve their twin goals of intimidating Republicans in general and destroying the Negro militia forces.

Intimidation of the Republicans took many forms. Parades and other public demonstrations of force were common occurrences and were attended by league members in full military regalia.[33] In the field of politics, several maneuvers were employed, the general policy being outlined in the instruction that "every Democrat must feel

[31] S. Rep. 527, 44th Cong., 1st Sess., p. 97.

[32] *Report of the Adjutant General of the State of South Carolina, 1874*, p. 6.

[33] Smedes, *A Southern Planter*, p. 230; Garner, *Reconstruction in Mississippi*, p. 374; S. Rep. 527, 44th Cong., 1st Sess., p. 279.

honor bound to control the vote of at least one Negro, by
intimidation, purchase, keeping him away, or as each
individual may determine how he may best accomplish
it."[34] Republican meetings were attended by White Liners
who threatened to break up the gatherings and often attempted to do so.[35] In some cases, particular Negroes were
singled out for pre-election visits and were subjected to
extremely harsh treatment.[36] Rifle companies were also
active at election time, sometimes resorting to force and
fraud to carry the day.[37] These and other methods of intimidation proved quite successful.

The White Leagues also struck forceful blows directly at
the Negro militia. Many of the race riots that took place
between whites and the militia were deliberately planned.
A member of a South Carolina rifle company confessed
that "it had been the settled purpose of the leading white
men . . . to seize the first opportunity that the negroes
might offer them to provoke a riot and teach the negroes
a lesson."[38]

Clashes took place in Louisiana, Mississippi, and South
Carolina. The last important one, which erupted in Hamburg, South Carolina, in early July, 1876, furnishes an
interesting study of a deliberately incited race riot. On
July 4, while marching "company front" down the main
street of town, the Negro militia company at Hamburg,

[34] Campaign instruction published by M. W. Gary of South Carolina in 1876, quoted in Simkins and Woody, *South Carolina during
Reconstruction*, pp. 564–69.

[35] Lynch, *Facts of Reconstruction*, p. 141; S. Rep. 527, 44th Cong.,
1st Sess., p. 837.

[36] H. W. Warren, *Reminiscences of a Mississippi Carpet-Bagger*,
p. 71.

[37] J. Meek to Adelbert Ames, November 2, 1875, Ames Papers.

[38] B. R. Tillman, *The Struggles of '76*, p. 17. (Pamphlet in the possession of the author.)

under the command of Doc Adams, attempted to force two white men in a buggy off the thoroughfare. An argument followed, but eventually the whites were allowed to pass. On the following day, the white men swore out a warrant for Adams' arrest, and trial was set for July 8. On that day, General M. C. Butler and his Sweetwater Sabre Club from Edgefield appeared in court, and one member of the group admitted that the purpose of the visit was "to provoke a row, and if one did not offer, we were to make one." Adams' failure to appear furnished the necessary pretext. General Butler journeyed across the state line to Augusta, where he managed to borrow a cannon, returned hastily to Hamburg, and assumed command of his troops.

In the meantime, Adams and his militiamen had gathered in the Sibley Building, which served as their armory. The Butler forces advanced upon the armory and demanded the surrender of all guns in storage there. When the militia captain refused to comply with this demand, fighting broke out. One of the whites was killed in the first volley; and when the Butler forces opened fire with their cannon, the Negroes hastily left the building. Thirty or forty militiamen were subsequently captured and placed under guard in the "Ring," an encampment near the railroad tracks. In the excitement that followed, several Negroes were murdered; five of the prisoners in the "Ring" were shot down within full view of their comrades.[39] Since the avowed purpose of their "visit" to Hamburg was "to strike terror,"[40] the members of Sweetwater Sabre Club

[39] Accounts of the Hamburg affair can be found in the following works: S. Misc. Doc. 48, Vol. I, 44th Cong., 2d Sess., pp. 33–34; Tillman, *The Struggles of '76*, p. 15; Reynolds, *Reconstruction in South Carolina*, pp. 344–47; *Anderson* (S.C.) *Intelligencer*, July 13, 1876.

[40] Tillman, *The Struggles of '76*, p. 24.

were able to return home secure in the knowledge that their mission had been accomplished. In spite of the fulminations of the Northern press, which launched a frenzied denunciation of "Sitting Bull Butler and His Edgefield Sioux,"[41] the perpetrators of the Hamburg slaughter were never punished.

Deliberate acts of violence were often carried out with the aid and co-operation of other companies from either neighboring counties or nearby states. During the Vicksburg troubles of 1874, a steamer was sent upriver to Yazoo City to transport arms loaned by White Liners there.[42] Out-of-state aid was quite common, as well. During the campaign of 1875 in Mississippi, whites from Alabama made frequent excursions across the line to aid their neighbors. G. K. Chase, sent to Mississippi by the United States Attorney General, reported to his superior that "an invasion from Alabama is imminent,"[43] and a Mobile newspaper urged that "Democratic and Conservative young men organize bands of minute men in every county" to aid their neighbors.[44] Governor Ames received a complaint from a Negro leader in Macon, Mississippi, that "the Alabama white people was out here on 25th of August AD 1875 killing up black people."[45] A white company from Helena, Arkansas, joined with the Conservative forces during the Friar's Point affair in Mississippi,[46] and some fifty or sixty Georgia whites under the leadership of a man named Dunn traveled from Augusta to Hamburg to "help relieve"

[41] Cited in Reynolds, *Reconstruction in South Carolina*, p. 347.
[42] Morgan, *Yazoo*, p. 440.
[43] George K. Chase to Attorney General Edwards Pierrepont, October 27, 1875, Ames Papers.
[44] Excerpt from *Mobile* (Ala.) *Register*, quoted in Morgan, *Yazoo*, p. 479.
[45] E. C. Walker to Adelbert Ames, August 26, 1875, Ames Papers.
[46] *New York Herald*, October 6, 1875.

the state of South Carolina.[47] A group of 160 armed whites from Louisiana crossed the Mississippi River to participate in the Vicksburg riot,[48] and the following telegram from Trinity, Texas, indicated that additional support from more distant areas could be counted upon:[49]

To President Board of Supervisors: Do you want any men? Can raise good crowd within twenty four hours to kill out your negroes.

White Line activity caused much uneasiness among loyal Republicans. Appeals to their leaders were numerous. Governor Ames received many appeals similar in tone to this one from his Negro supporters: "We ask you for our protection or helpe some way or erther, knowing that you are our govnor and the only help for us."[50] Even President Grant received messages telling of deplorable conditions and requesting help:[51]

Honored Sir: This letter is from a Poor freedman   I write to Let you no about times down this way the rebels are outrageous   In our city they have about fifteen Hundred Riffles scattered about in difrent hourse and they sit up every night to watch them and they say the first chance they get they are going to kill the Dam leaders of the Republican party and all the dam Yankeis and niggers and that is just what they are doing. . . .

Several attempts were made to curtail or destroy the growing White Line movement. Governors resorted to issuing proclamations demanding the disbandment of the

[47] S. Misc. Doc. 48, Vol. I, 44th Cong., 2d Sess., p. 675.

[48] H.R. Rep. 265, 43d Cong., 2d Sess., p. ix.

[49] Telegram from J. G. Gates and A. H. Mason, December 12, 1874, quoted in *ibid.*

[50] W. K. Jones to Adelbert Ames, September 10, 1875, quoted in S. Rep. 527, 44th Cong., 1st Sess., p. 19.

[51] S. Misc. Doc. 48, Vol. III, 44th Cong., 2d Sess., p. 99.

rifle clubs. Ames took this step during the campaign of 1875 in Mississippi,[52] and Governor Chamberlain followed suit in South Carolina.[53] The proclamations were never effective. South Carolinians merely ignored Chamberlain's words, while Mississippians were openly defiant: "Ames emerged from his hole the other day and staid out long enough to say to the companies . . . 'disband.' But at the present writing they are not disbanding worth a cent, nor do they have any idea of doing such a thing."[54]

White Line violence in South Carolina reached such alarming proportions that President Grant was forced to issue a presidential proclamation directing the rifle companies to disperse within three days.[55] The terms of the proclamation were obeyed in letter though not in spirit. The companies officially disbanded but were immediately reorganized under such innocuous titles as the First Baptist Church Sewing Circle, the Hampton and Tilden Musical Club, and the Allendale Mounted Baseball Club, whose roster of players contained the impressive total of 150 names.[56] Measures aimed at destroying the companies were thus effectively nullified.

The White Line movement was eminently successful in accomplishing its aim of political restoration through force. Republican voters in general and Radical politicians in particular were in agreement with the sentiments expressed by one of their number: "We have been slumbering on a volcano. . . . It is no longer with them the number of votes

[52] Garner, *Reconstruction in Mississippi*, p. 378.

[53] *Anderson* (S.C.) *Intelligencer*, October 12, 1876.

[54] Excerpt from *Yazoo City* (Miss.) *Herald*, quoted in Morgan, *Yazoo*, p. 470.

[55] Proclamation issued October 17, 1876, copy in *Appleton's Annual Cyclopaedia, 1876*, p. 721.

[56] Simkins and Woody, *South Carolina during Reconstruction*, p. 509.

but the number of guns."[57] Political action of rifle companies was directly responsible for Democratic victories in
Mississippi and South Carolina; and although final tri-
umph did not come in Louisiana until 1877, the White
Leagues contributed their part by maintaining considerable pressure on local Republicans.

Equally successful was the policy aimed at smashing
remaining Negro militia units. The mere appearance of
these armed military counterforces caused many militia
units to disband voluntarily. Others were harassed, an-
noyed, and intimidated into ineffectiveness, while still
others were destroyed by force. From the ranks of the
White Line movement came the men who engaged Negro
militia forces in the bloody affairs at Vicksburg, Clinton,
and Hamburg, where the whites inaugurated a policy of
disbandment through extermination.

[57] John Meek to Adelbert Ames, November 2, 1875, Ames Papers.

X. Conclusion

JUDGED BY ITS ACCOMPLISHMENTS, as compared with its
professed aims, the Negro militia movement was a dismal
failure. By 1877, it was apparent for all to see that the
last of the Radical state governments were doomed and
that individual militia units had been destroyed, disbanded,
or rendered militarily ineffective. In order to understand
the failure of the militia movement, one must also understand certain aspects of the campaign of violence waged
against it. Why were the whites able to prevail by armed
force over the Negro militia? What were the real reasons
that caused the whites to turn to such extreme measures?

The ultimate victory of the whites in the struggle was
not due entirely to their own aggressive action. These
had their effect, to be sure; but it is unlikely that such
policies as retaliation against individual militiamen or
even the creation of White Line rifle companies would have
been sufficient in themselves to guarantee victory had there
not been a basic error in strategy on the part of Radical
leaders that seriously weakened the militia movement from
within. This error was the failure to employ the militia
forces to the full extent of their power, and the fault lies
squarely with the Radical governors. Even in exceptional
cases where executives favored maximum utility of their
troops, they received much advice to the contrary. Governor
Clayton, of Arkansas, was warned by no less a person than
his own adjutant general against using Negro troops "except in case of extreme necessity."[1] A good deal of the reluctance to employ Negro soldiers stemmed directly from

---

[1] Keyes Danforth to Powell Clayton, December 12, 1868, quoted in
Clayton, *Aftermath in Arkansas*, p. 119.

lack of confidence in their military prowess,[2] but this was not the sole reason. Governor Brownlow, for instance, expressed his displeasure at both the freedom with which Negro militiamen used their guns and their general attitude toward whites.[3] However, the main deterrent was fear. Haunted by the specter of race war, governors temporized and satisfied themselves with half-measures.[4] In Alabama, numerous applications from "colored fellow citizens from Mobile, Selma, and Montgomery" requesting permission to organize militia companies were turned down by the adjutant general on explicit orders from Governor Lewis.[5] Ames hesitated a long while before finally calling up his Negro troops in Mississippi, and, by his own admission, the delay was prompted by his fear that arming the militia would cause the state "to drift into a war of races."[6] When an outbreak of violence occurred in Jackson County, Florida, in late 1869, many demands were made on Governor Reed to send a loyal militia force there to quell the disturbance. Reed, fearful of the consequences of such action, agreed to raise a Negro regiment for the purpose, provided the leading Radical agitator, named Purman, would command it. His offer was speedily declined.[7] This reluctance to mount an all-out offensive not only sapped the strength of the militia movement but also proved that

[2] J. C. Delavigne, "The Troubles in the South," *The Southern Magazine*, Vol. IX (1875), p. 517.

[3] Coulter, *Brownlow*, p. 290.

[4] One Negro historian flatly states that "the Reconstruction governors were afraid to use these militia forces lest they start a race war. . . ." (W. E. B. DuBois, *Black Reconstruction*, p. 690.)

[5] *Annual Report of the Adjutant General of the State of Alabama, 1873*, p. 3.

[6] Adelbert Ames to A. T. Morgan, August 14, 1874, Ames Papers.

[7] Davis, *Reconstruction in Florida*, p. 577.

Radical leaders were either ignorant of or unwilling to subscribe to the political theorem that "Social Revolutions are not accomplished by force, unless that force is over-whelming, merciless, and continued over a long period."[8]

Another source of weakness in the Negro militia forces was the fact that they were, in a very real sense, abandoned by the national Republican administration. This abandon-ment was reflected in such actions as Grant's refusal to intervene in Texas and Mississippi at crucial periods of the struggles in those states. However, the apparent betrayal came about as a natural result of circumstances rather than as a deliberate plot to desert the Negro in his extremity. The cooling off of the Grant administration was essentially a reaction to the pressure of changing Northern public opin-ion. It is true that when Governor E. J. Davis, of Texas, appealed to the President for troops his request was refused, and he was piously advised "to yield to the verdict of the people."[9] It is no less true that at the same time Grant was being plagued by an unfavorable reaction in public opinion that not only raised questions concerning Southern policy in general but also levied the charge of "Caesarism" against the President personally. When Ames asked for Federal troops during the campaign of 1875 in Mississippi, he was refused them with the terse but true comment that "the whole public are tired of the annual autumnal out-breaks in the south."[10] Ames later remarked with some bitterness that "this flippant utterance . . . was the way the executive branch of the national government announced that it had decided that the reconstruction acts of Congress

[8] Wharton, *The Negro in Mississippi*, p. 198.

[9] Clarence R. Wharton, *Texas under Many Flags*, p. 205; *New York Herald*, January 13, 1874.

[10] Cited in Wharton, *The Negro in Mississippi*, p. 194.

were a failure."[11] A further indication that the Northern people had grown weary of the Reconstruction experiment can be seen in the fierce reaction following on the heels of General Sheridan's famous "banditti" message sent from New Orleans early in 1875. Several Northern state legislatures censured the action, and many protest meetings were held in Northern cities.[12]

As Northern public opinion continued to apply restraining pressures on the Grant administration, Southern whites began to be less fearful of intervention by the federal government and grew bolder in their use of violence at the very time when militia forces were becoming increasingly vulnerable as a result of internal weakness.

Since the militia was destroyed by means of a carefully planned and well executed campaign of violence, it is necessary to inquire into the reasons why Southern whites resorted to such extreme measures. Unquestionably, the cost of the program generated a great deal of resentment. A few figures will be sufficient to illustrate this point. In Texas, Limestone and Freestone counties were assessed $36,000 to pay costs of martial law proclaimed within their boundaries.[13] The short but fierce Kirk-Holden War cost North Carolinians almost $75,000;[14] militia participation in only one election in Tennessee cost over $93,000.[15] In addition to the enormous expenses incident to maintaining the metropolitan police in New Orleans,[16] the Louisiana Legislature appropriated an additional $100,000 for

11 Adelbert Ames to E. B. Andrews, May 24, 1895, Garner Papers.
12 Lonn, *Reconstruction in Louisiana*, pp. 304–305.
13 Herbert, *Why the Solid South?* pp. 376–77.
14 Hamilton, *Reconstruction in North Carolina*, p. 531.
15 Coulter, *Brownlow*, p. 339.
16 Herbert, *Why the Solid South?* p. 400.

support of the state militia.[17] Arkansas spent $330,000 during the martial-law period of 1868–69,[18] and another $200,000 as a result of the Brooks-Baxter War.[19] An investigating committee of the South Carolina Legislature fixed the cost of enrolling and arming the militia of that state at $375,000.[20]

Not only were appropriated funds used to pay troops and purchase the wherewithal to make war, but also this money invariably became involved in the too-prevalent corruption of the period. Payroll-padding was so common a practice that Governor Moses admitted under oath that not one-fourth of the persons listed on the South Carolina rolls at one period rendered any military service.[21]

Through militia claims commissions, vast sums of money passed into the pockets of persons who had the good fortune to be recognized as avid supporters of the incumbent administration and the willingness to swear to a falsehood. In Arkansas, such a commission was created by the Legislature as a result of Governor Clayton's urging.[22] During the single year in which it functioned, it disbursed over $120,000 of Arkansas taxpayers' money. It is interesting to note that the commissioner himself collected on at least two claims.[23]

Governor Scott used $50,000 of militia money to bribe

[17] Bowers, *The Tragic Era*, p. 365; Lonn, *Reconstruction in Louisiana*, p. 65.

[18] Staples, *Reconstruction in Arkansas*, pp. 304–305.

[19] Testimony of James R. Berry, Arkansas state auditor, H.R. Rep. 2, 43d Cong., 2d Sess., p. 505.

[20] Reynolds, *Reconstruction in South Carolina*, p. 177.

[21] *Report of the Joint Investigating Committee on Public Frauds in South Carolina, 1877–78*, p. 677.

[22] Clayton, *Aftermath in Arkansas*, pp. 165–66.

[23] Staples, *Reconstruction in Arkansas*, p. 303.

three South Carolina legislators in order to escape impeachment,[24] and his Adjutant General, Franklin J. Moses, Jr., reportedly made the greatest single financial killing of his entire career from militia funds, a significant statement in view of his career,[25] which was so spectacular that a few of his antics bear relating. On one occasion he was sent north by Governor Scott to purchase rifles for the state. By the business technique known as the "kickback," he received a fat sum from the supplier.[26] His biggest deal involved guns that had been furnished to South Carolina by the federal government. Although the guns were in good working order, Moses negotiated a contract amounting to $165,000 to have them altered to breech-loading rifles. The alteration price per gun was greater than the cost of a new gun from the same company making the alterations. Not only was an estimated $75,000 swindled in this particular deal,[27] but, according to an employee in the Adjutant General's office, the guns were actually less serviceable after the costly alteration.[28]

The office of adjutant general, through which militia forces were commanded, became little more than a sinecure with a handsome salary that could be used as a reward to the politically faithful. Nepotism was not uncommon. Governor Brownlow, for example, found his son to be admirably fitted for the job, and he subsequently ele-

[24] Reynolds, *Reconstruction in South Carolina*, p. 173.

[25] R. H. Woody, "Franklin J. Moses, Jr., Scalawag Governor of South Carolina, 1872–74," *The North Carolina Historical Review*, Vol. X (April, 1933), p. 119.

[26] *Report of the Joint Investigating Committee on Public Frauds in South Carolina, 1877–78*, p. 672.

[27] *Proceedings of the Tax-Payer's Convention of South Carolina, 1874*, p. 95.

[28] Testimony of John B. Dennis, *Report of the Joint Investigating Committee on Public Frauds in South Carolina, 1877–78*, p. 680.

vated a nephew, Sam Hunt, to the office.[29] Governor Davis likewise filled the vacancy in Texas with a near relation, F. L. Britton.[30]

In addition to the resentment resulting from the costs and frauds of the militia movement, considerable bitterness was created by militia activities. Although this phase of their history has been discussed in Chapter III, it should be reiterated here that the Negro militia was unwisely handled.[31] Their continued activity in politics, their depredations, and their minor social offenses undoubtedly increased the ill-feeling of the whites and must be considered as factors leading to their ultimate destruction.

To the casual observer, the catalogue of offenses committed by militiamen, plus the costs and frauds involved, might seem sufficient to explain the failure of the militia movement. But any such conclusion would be an oversimplification. One must be very careful in any analysis of factors explaining Southern attitudes and reactions to distinguish between actual and imaginary wrongs. In this particular case, the actual wrongs—the petty annoyances and the depredations of the militia—merely served to aggravate a situation that from the very beginning was intolerable to many Southern whites because of the racial implications. The South during Reconstruction was not yet ready to acquiesce in the pious sentiments of the congressman who declared that on that "last great day when the horn shall sound" the question would not be whether he is "a black sheep or a white sheep, but whether it is good

[29] Coulter, *Brownlow*, p. 267.

[30] Clarence P. Denman, "The Office of Adjutant-General in Texas, 1835–81," *Southwestern Historical Quarterly*, Vol. XXVIII (1924), pp. 302–23.

[31] Alrutheus A. Taylor, *The Negro in South Carolina during Reconstruction*, p. 190. (Hereafter cited as *The Negro in South Carolina*.)

mutton."[32] For even had the militia refrained from committing a single act antagonistic to the whites, in all probability they would still have been destroyed. A Negro historian cuts right through to the heart of the matter with this statement: "The very fact that the Negro wore a uniform and thereby enjoyed certain rights was an affront to most southern whites."[33]

The racial affront was at the core of the white man's hatred of the Negro militia. From racial bitterness it is but a short step to racial conflict; consequently, that strain of violence which runs with such persistence through the course of Southern history once again erupted.

In retrospect, it appears fairly obvious that the Radicals, from the very beginning of their militia experiment, faced a paradox. Confronted with the stern realities of political self-preservation, they found it imperative to create a protective force, which, owing to peculiar local conditions, developed into a Negro militia. It is ironic that the organization of this protective force, because of its racial implications, actually aided in the destruction of the very political movement it was created to protect.

[32] Speech of Representative Samuel S. Cox of New York, July 18, 1876, quoted in *Congressional Record*, Vol. IV, 44th Cong., 1st Sess., p. 4707.

[33] E. Franklin Frazier, *The Negro in the United States*, p. 145. Another Negro historian confirms this belief by stating that "the very sight of the Negro in military uniform enraged the native whites. . . ." (Taylor, *The Negro in South Carolina*, p. 190.)

Bibliography

Manuscript Material

Adjutant General's Office, files, state of Arkansas. Little Rock, Ark.: Arkansas Historical Commission. (Several volumes, including general and special orders relating to Arkansas State Guards and miscellaneous letter books.)

Adjutant General's Office, files, state of Tennessee. Nashville, Tenn.: Department of Archives. (Orders and correspondence of Adjutant-General James P. Brownlow and General Joseph A. Cooper plus several letter books of Tennessee State Guards.)

Adjutant General's Office, files, state of Texas. Austin, Texas: Texas State Library, Archives. (Letters, commissions, musters, and orders relating to Texas Militia.)

Alcorn, James L.: Papers. Chapel Hill, N.C.: University of North Carolina, Southern History Collection.

Ames, Adelbert: Papers. Jackson, Miss.: Mississippi Department of Archives and History. (Voluminous collection consisting of official letter books, eleven boxes of miscellaneous letters and documents, and official records of Ames's term as governor.)

Brownlow, William G.: Papers. Nashville, Tenn.: Tennessee Department of Archives. (Several letter books dealing with period of militia activity in Tennessee.)

Clayton, Powell: Papers. Little Rock, Ark.: Arkansas Historical Commission. (Approximately 1,000 letters written during period of militia activity.)

Garner, James W.: Papers. Jackson, Miss.: Mississippi Department of Archives and History.

Grant, Ulysses S.: Papers. Washington: Library of Congress, Manuscripts Division.

Holden, W. W.: Papers. Raleigh, N.C.: North Carolina Department of Archives and History. (Several boxes of records and letter books dealing with the period of the Kirk-Holden War.)

Johnson, Andrew: Papers. Washington: Library of Congress, Manuscripts Division.

Kellogg, William Pitt: Papers. Baton Rouge, La.: Louisiana State University, Department of Archives.

Moses, Franklin J., Jr.: Papers. Columbia, S.C.: South Carolina Historical Commission.

Scott, Robert K.: Papers. Columbia, S.C.: South Carolina Historical Commission.

Sheridan, Philip H.: Papers. Washington: Library of Congress, Manuscripts Division. (Many interesting letters and messages written during the period.)

Sherman, William T.: Papers. Washington: Library of Congress, Manuscripts Division.

South Carolina Military Affairs File. Columbia, S.C.: South Carolina Historical Commission. (Several thousand relevant items—letters, accounts, records, reports, orders, and petitions—relating to the South Carolina Militia in the period 1866–77.)

Warmoth, Henry Clay: Papers. Chapel Hill, N.C.: University of North Carolina, Southern History Collection.

Official Records and Documents—Federal Government

Note: All documents listed below were issued by the Government Printing Office, Washington.

Annual Report of the Secretary of War. 1866–77.

Congressional Globe. 1865–73.

Congressional Record. 1873–77.

Executive Documents of the House of Representatives. 1865–76.

Executive Documents of the Senate. 1865–76.

Journal of the House of Representatives. 39th–44th Cong.

Miscellaneous Documents of the House of Representatives. 1865–76.

Miscellaneous Documents of the Senate. 1865–76.

Reports of the Committees of the House of Representatives. 1865–76.

Reports of the Committees of the Senate. 1865–76.

Official Records and Documents—State Governments

Acts of the State of Tennessee for the Year 1865. Nashville, Tenn., 1865.

Annual Report of the Adjutant General of the State of Louisiana, 1870–74. New Orleans, La., 1871–75.

Report of the Adjutant General of Alabama, 1873. Montgomery, Ala., 1873.

Report of the Adjutant General of Arkansas, 1864–1866. Washington, 1867.

Report of the Adjutant and Inspector General of South Carolina, 1868. Charleston, S.C., 1868.

Report of Evidence Taken before the Military Committee, 35th General Assembly, State of Tennessee, 1868. Nashville, Tenn., 1868.

Report of the Joint Committee of the General Assembly of Louisiana on the Conduct of the Late Elections and the Conditions of Peace and Order in the State. New Orleans, La., 1868.

Report of the Joint Investigating Committee on Public Frauds, General Assembly of South Carolina, 1877–1878. Columbia, S.C., 1878.

Newspapers

Anderson (S.C.) *Intelligencer.*
Austin (Texas) *Daily Democratic Statesman.*
Charleston (S.C.) *Daily News.*
Columbia (S.C.) *Daily Register.*
Hinds County (Miss.) *Gazette.*
Jackson (Miss.) *Weekly Clarion.*
Little Rock (Ark.) *Daily Arkansas Gazette.*
Nashville (Tenn.) *Daily Press and Times.*
Nashville (Tenn.) *Republican Banner.*
Nashville (Tenn.) *Union and Dispatch.*
New Orleans (La.) *Picayune.*
New York Herald.
New York Times.
New York Tribune.

Raleigh (N.C.) *Daily Sentinel.*
Salem (N.C.) *People's Press.*
Van Buren (Ark.) *Free Press.*

Periodicals

DeBow's Review. 1866–70.
The Galaxy. 1866–74.
Harper's Weekly. 1865–76.
The Independent. 1873–76.
The Nation. 1865–76.
The XIX Century. 1870.
The Southern Magazine. 1871–76.

Memoirs, Autobiographies, and Contemporary Accounts

Alvord, John W.: *Letters from the South Relating to the Freedmen.* Washington: Howard University Press, 1870.
Andrews, Sidney: *The South since the War.* Boston: Ticknor and Fields, 1866.
Avary, Myrta L.: *Dixie after the War.* New York: Doubleday, 1906.
Benham, George C.: *A Year of Wreck.* New York: Harper, 1880.
Blaine, James G.: *Twenty Years of Congress.* 2 vols. Norwich, Conn.: Henry Bill, 1886.
Campbell, Sir George: *White and Black: The Outcome of a Visit to the United States.* New York: R. Worthington, 1879.
Childs, Arney R. (ed.): *The Private Journal of Henry William Ravenel, 1859–1887.* Columbia, S.C.: University of South Carolina Press, 1947.
Clayton, Powell: *The Aftermath of the Civil War in Arkansas.* New York: Neale, 1915.
Cox, S. S.: *Three Decades of Federal Legislation.* Providence, R.I.: Reid, 1885.

De Forest, John William: *A Union Officer in the Reconstruction.* New Haven, Conn.: Yale University Press, 1948.

Dixon, William H.: *White Conquest.* 2 vols. London: Chatto and Windus, 1876.

Harrell, John M.: *The Brooks and Baxter War.* St. Louis, Mo.: Slawson Printing Co., 1893.

Higginson, Thomas W.: *Army Life in a Black Regiment.* Boston: Fields and Osgood, 1870.

Holden, William W.: *Memoirs.* Durham, N.C.: Seeman Printing, 1911.

Kennaway, John H.: *On Sherman's Track: The South after the War.* London: Seeley, Jackson, and Halliday, 1867.

King, Edward: *The Great South.* Hartford, Conn.: American, 1875.

Leigh, Frances Butler: *Ten Years on a Georgia Plantation.* London: Bentley and Son, 1883.

Leland, John A.: *A Voice from South Carolina.* Charleston, S.C.: Walker, Evans, and Cogswell, 1879.

Lynch, James D.: *Kemper County Vindicated and a Peep at Radical Rule in Mississippi.* New York: Hale and Sons, 1879.

Lynch, John R.: *The Facts of Reconstruction.* New York: Neale, 1913.

McClure, Alexander K.: *Recollections of Half a Century.* Salem, Mass.: Salem, 1902.

Mills, W. W.: *Forty Years at El Paso.* El Paso, Texas: Mills, 1901.

Morgan, A. T.: *Yazoo: On the Picket Line of Freedom in the South.* Washington: Morgan, 1884.

Nordhoff, Charles: *The Cotton States in the Spring and Summer of 1875.* New York: Appleton, 1876.

Pike, James S.: *The Prostrate State: South Carolina under Negro Government.* New York: Appleton, 1874.

Reid, Whitelaw: *After the War: A Southern Tour.* Cincinnati, Ohio: Moore, Wilstach and Baldwin, 1866.

Shuften, John T.: *A Colored Man's Exposition of the Acts and Doings of the Republican Party South.* Jacksonville, Fla.: Gibson and Dennis, 1877.

Smedes, Susan Dabney: *A Southern Planter.* London: John Murray, 1889.

Somers, Robert: *The Southern States since the War.* New York: Macmillan, 1871.

Stearns, Charles: *The Black Man of the South and the Rebels.* New York: American News Co., 1872.

Tourgee, Albion W.: *An Appeal to Caesar.* New York: Fords, Howard and Hulbert, 1884.

———: *The Invisible Empire.* New York: Fords, Howard and Hulbert, 1879.

Trowbridge, John T.: *A Picture of the Desolated States and the Work of Restoration, 1865–1868.* Hartford, Conn.: L. Stebbins, 1868.

Wallace, John: *Carpetbag Rule in Florida.* Jacksonville, Fla.: Da Costa, 1888.

Warmoth, Henry Clay: *War, Politics and Reconstruction: Stormy Days in Louisiana.* New York: Macmillan, 1930.

Warren, Henry W.: *Reminiscences of a Mississippi Carpet-Bagger.* Worcester, Mass.: Davis, 1914.

Wells, James M.: *The Chisolm Massacre: A Picture of "Home Rule" in Mississippi.* Washington: Chisolm Monument Association, 1878.

General Works and Special Studies—Published Sources and Reference Works

American Annual Cyclopaedia and Register of Important Events. 1868–76. New York: D. Appleton, 1869–77.

Fleming, Walter L.: *Documentary History of Reconstruction.* Cleveland, Ohio: Arthur H. Clark, 1906.

McPherson, E.: *The Political History of the United States of America during the Period of Reconstruction, 1865–1870.* Washington: Solomons and Chapman, 1875.

Richardson, James D.: *A Compilation of the Messages and Papers of the Presidents, 1789–1907.* Washington: Government Printing Office, 1908, Vols. 6, 7.

Rowland, Dunbar: *Encyclopedia of Mississippi History.* Madison, Wis.: Selwyn A. Brant, 1907.

General Works and Special Studies—State Histories of Reconstruction

Caskey, Willie M.: *Secession and Restoration of Louisiana.* Baton Rouge, La.: Louisiana State University Press, 1938.

Davis, William W.: *The Civil War and Reconstruction in Florida.* New York: Columbia University Press, 1913.

Eckenrode, Hamilton J.: *The Political History of Virginia during the Reconstruction.* Baltimore, Md.: Johns Hopkins Press, 1904.

Fertig, James W.: *The Secession and Reconstruction of Tennessee.* Chicago: University of Chicago Press, 1898.

Ficklen, John R.: *History of Reconstruction in Louisiana (through 1868).* Baltimore, Md.: Johns Hopkins Press, 1910.

Fleming, Walter L.: *Civil War and Reconstruction in Alabama.* New York: Columbia University Press, 1905.

Garner, James W.: *Reconstruction in Mississippi.* New York: Macmillan, 1901.

Hamilton, Joseph G. de R.: *Reconstruction in North Carolina.* New York: Columbia University Press, 1914.

Lonn, Ella: *Reconstruction in Louisiana after 1868.* New York: Putnam's, 1918.

Patton, James W.: *Unionism and Reconstruction in Tennessee, 1860–1869.* Chapel Hill, N.C.: University of North Carolina Press, 1934.

Ramsdell, Charles W.: *Reconstruction in Texas.* New York: Columbia University Press, 1910.

Reynolds, John S.: *Reconstruction in South Carolina, 1865–1877.* Columbia, S.C.: State, 1905.

Simkins, F. B., and R. H. Woody: *South Carolina during Reconstruction.* Chapel Hill, N.C.: University of North Carolina Press, 1932.

Staples, Thomas S.: *Reconstruction in Arkansas, 1862–1874.* New York: Columbia University Press, 1923.

Thomas, David Y.: *Arkansas in War and Reconstruction.* Little Rock, Ark.: Central, 1926.

Thompson, C. Mildred: *Reconstruction in Georgia.* New York: Columbia University Press, 1915.

General Works and Special Studies—General Works

Allen, James S.: *Reconstruction, the Battle for Democracy, 1865–1876.* New York: International, 1937.

Allen, Walter: *Governor Chamberlain's Administration in South Carolina.* New York: Putnam, 1888.

Ball, William W.: *The State That Forgot.* Indianapolis, Ind.: Bobbs-Merrill, 1932.

Bowers, Claude G.: *The Tragic Era.* Boston: Houghton Mifflin, 1929.

Brewer, J. Mason: *Negro Legislators of Texas.* Dallas, Texas: Mathis, 1935.

Brewster, James: *Sketches of Southern Mystery, Treason and Murder.* N.p., n.d.

Brown, A. J.: *History of Newton County, Mississippi (1834–1894).* Jackson, Miss.: Clarion-Ledger, 1894.

Brown, William G.: *The Lower South in American History.* New York: Macmillan, 1902.

Buck, Paul H.: *The Road to Reunion, 1865–1900.* Boston: Little, Brown, 1937.

Burgess, John W.: *Reconstruction and the Constitution, 1866–1876.* New York: Scribner, 1905.

Cable, George W.: *The Silent South.* New York: Scribner, 1885.

Cash, William T.: *History of the Democratic Party in Florida.* Tallahassee, Fla.: Democratic Historical Foundation, 1936.

Chandler, Julian A. C. (ed.): *The South in the Building of the Nation.* Richmond, Va.: Southern Historical Publication Society, 1909.

Coulter, E. Merton: *The South during Reconstruction.* Baton Rouge, La.: Louisiana State University Press, 1947.

———: *William G. Brownlow: Fighting Parson of the Southern Highlands.* Chapel Hill, N.C.: University of North Carolina Press, 1937.

Davidson, Donald: *The Tennessee.* 2 vols. New York: Rinehart, 1948.

DuBois, W. E. B.: *Black Reconstruction.* New York: Harcourt, Brace, 1935.

DuBose, John W.: *Alabama's Tragic Decade, 1865–1874.* Birmingham, Ala.: Webb, 1940.

Dunning, William A.: *Essays on the Civil War and Reconstruction.* New York: Macmillan, 1898.

————: *Reconstruction Political and Economic, 1865–1877.* New York: Harper, 1907.

Eckenrode, Hamilton J.: *Rutherford B. Hayes, Statesman of Reunion.* New York: Dodd, Mead, 1930.

————, and B. Conrad: *James Longstreet, Lee's War Horse.* Chapel Hill, N.C.: University of North Carolina Press, 1936.

Fleming, Walter L.: *The Sequel of Appomattox.* New Haven, Conn.: Yale University Press, 1919.

Fletcher, John Gould: *Arkansas.* Chapel Hill, N.C.: University of North Carolina Press, 1947.

Fortier, Alcée: *A History of Louisiana.* New York: Manzi, Joyant, 1904.

Frazier, E. Franklin: *The Negro in the United States.* New York: Macmillan, 1949.

Hamilton, Peter J.: *The Reconstruction Period.* Philadelphia: Barrie, 1905.

Henderson, Archibald: *North Carolina, the Old State and the New.* 2 vols. Chicago: Lewis, 1941.

Henry, Robert S.: *"First with the Most" Forrest.* New York: Bobbs-Merrill, 1944.

————: *The Story of Reconstruction.* New York: Bobbs-Merrill, 1938.

Herbert, Hilary A.: *Why the Solid South?* Baltimore, Md.: R. H. Woodward, 1890.

Hesseltine, William B.: *Ulysses S. Grant, Politician.* New York: Dodd, Mead, 1935.

Horn, Stanley F.: *Invisible Empire: The Story of the Ku Klux Klan, 1866–1871.* Boston: Houghton Mifflin, 1939.

Jarrell, Hampton M.: *Wade Hampton and the Negro.* Columbia, S.C.: University of South Carolina Press, 1949.

Lester, J. C., and D. L. Wilson: *Ku Klux Klan.* New York: Neale, 1905.

Lewinson, Paul: *Race, Class and Party.* New York: Oxford University Press, 1932.

Lynch, Denis T.: *The Wild Seventies.* New York: Appleton-Century, 1941.

McGinty, Garnie W.: *Louisiana Redeemed: The Overthrow of Carpetbag Rule, 1876–1880*. New Orleans, La.: Pelican, 1941.

Mayes, Edward: *Lucius Q. C. Lamar: His Life, Times and Speeches, 1825–1893*. Nashville, Tenn.: Methodist Episcopal Church, South, 1896.

Milton, George F.: *The Age of Hate*. New York: Coward, McCann, 1930.

Oberholtzer, Ellis P.: *A History of the United States since the Civil War*. 5 vols. New York: Macmillan, 1926.

Peirce, Paul S.: *The Freedmen's Bureau*. Iowa City, Iowa: State University of Iowa, 1904.

Pollard, Edward A.: *The Lost Cause Regained*. New York: Carleton, 1868.

Randall, James G.: *The Civil War and Reconstruction*. New York: Heath, 1937.

Rhodes, James Ford: *History of the United States from the Compromise of 1850 to Final Restoration of Home Rule at the South in 1877*. 7 vols. New York: Macmillan, 1910.

Sanger, D. B., and T. R. Hay: *James Longstreet*. Baton Rouge, La.: Louisiana State University Press, 1952.

Sheppard, William A.: *Red Shirts Remembered*. Atlanta, Ga.: Ruralist Press, 1940.

Shugg, Roger W.: *Origins of Class Struggle in Louisiana*. Baton Rouge, La.: Louisiana State University Press, 1939.

Simkins, Francis B.: *A History of the South*. New York: Knopf, 1953.

———: *Pitchfork Ben Tillman, South Carolinian*. Baton Rouge, La.: Louisiana State University Press, 1944.

Stryker, Lloyd P.: *Andrew Johnson*. New York: Macmillan, 1929.

Swint, Henry Lee: *The Northern Teacher in the South, 1862–1870*. Nashville, Tenn.: Vanderbilt University, 1941.

Taylor, Alrutheus A.: *The Negro in the Reconstruction of Virginia*. Washington: Association for the Study of Negro Life and History, 1926.

———: *The Negro in South Carolina during Reconstruction*. Washington: Association for the Study of Negro Life and History, 1924.

————: *The Negro in Tennessee, 1865–1880.* Washington: Associated Publishers, 1941.

Thompson, Henry T.: *Ousting the Carpetbaggers from South Carolina.* Columbia, S.C.: Bryan, 1927.

Wellman, Manly W.: *Giant in Gray.* New York: Scribners, 1949.

Wells, Edward L.: *Hampton and Reconstruction.* Columbia, S.C.: State, 1907.

Wharton, Clarence R.: *Texas under Many Flags.* New York: American Historical Society, 1930.

Wharton, Vernon L.: *The Negro in Mississippi, 1865–1890.* Chapel Hill, N.C.: University of North Carolina Press, 1947.

Williams, Alfred B.: *Hampton and His Red Shirts.* Charleston, S.C.: Walker, Evans and Cogswell, 1935.

General Works and Special Studies—Articles

Beale, Howard K.: "On Rewriting Reconstruction History," *American Historical Review,* Vol. XLV (1940), pp. 807–27.

Brough, Charles H.: "The Clinton Riot," *Publications of the Mississippi Historical Society,* Vol. VI (1902), pp. 53–64.

Cypert, Eugene: "Constitutional Convention of 1868," *Publications of the Arkansas Historical Association,* Vol. IV (1917), pp. 7–57.

Delavigne, J. C.: "The Troubles in the South," *The Southern Magazine,* Vol. IX (1875), pp. 513–19.

Denman, Clarence P.: "The Office of Adjutant General in Texas, 1835–1881," *The Southwestern Historical Quarterly,* Vol. XXVIII (1924), pp. 302–23.

House, Albert V., Jr.: "Northern Congressional Democrats as Defenders of the South during Reconstruction," *The Journal of Southern History,* Vol. VI (February, 1940), pp. 46–71.

Johnson, Benjamin S.: "The Brooks-Baxter War," *Publications of the Arkansas Historical Association,* Vol. III (1908), pp. 122–74.

Johnston, Frank: "Conference between General George and Governor Ames," *Publications of the Mississippi Historical Society*, Vol. VI (1902), pp. 65–78.

Lestage, H. Oscar, Jr.: "The White League in Louisiana and its Participation in Reconstruction Riots," *The Louisiana Historical Quarterly*, Vol. XVIII (1935), pp. 617–95.

McNeily, John S.: "Climax and Collapse of Reconstruction in Mississippi, 1874–1896," *Publications of the Mississippi Historical Society*, Vol. XII (1912), pp. 283–474.

————: "The Enforcement Act of 1871 and the Ku Klux Klan in Mississippi," *Publications of the Mississippi Historical Society*, Vol. IX (1906), pp. 109–72.

————: "War and Reconstruction in Mississippi, 1863–1890," *Publications of the Mississippi Historical Society*, Vol. II (1918), pp. 165–536.

Pegram, W. H.: "A Ku Klux Raid and What Came of It," *Annual Publication of Historical Papers, Trinity College Historical Society*, Series 1 (1897), pp. 65–71.

Post, Louis F.: "A Carpetbagger in South Carolina," *Journal of Negro History*, Vol. X (1925), pp. 10–80.

Queener, Verton M.: "A Decade of East Tennessee Republicanism," *The East Tennessee Historical Society's Publications*, Vol. XIV (1942), pp. 59–86.

Rainwater, Percy L. (ed.): "The Autobiography of Benjamin Grubb Humphreys, August 26, 1808–December 20, 1882," *The Mississippi Valley Historical Review*, Vol. XXI (1934), pp. 231–54.

Reynolds, Thomas J., "The Pope County Militia War," *Publications of the Arkansas Historical Association*, Vol. II (1908), pp. 174–99.

Rose, U. M.: "Clayton's Aftermath of the Civil War in Arkansas," *Publications of the Arkansas Historical Association*, Vol. IV (1917), pp. 57–66.

Sharp, J. A.: "The Downfall of the Radicals in Tennessee," *The East Tennessee Historical Society's Publications*, Vol. V (1933), pp. 105–25.

Simkins, Francis B.: "The Ku Klux Klan in South Carolina, 1868–1871," *Journal of Negro History*, Vol. XII (1927), pp. 606–47.

————: "New Viewpoints of Southern Reconstruction," *Journal of Southern History*, Vol. V (1939), pp. 49–61.

Wesley, Charles H.: "The Employment of Negroes as Soldiers in the Confederate Army," *Journal of Negro History*, Vol. IV (1919), pp. 239–53.

Wheeler, T. B.: "Reminiscences of Reconstruction in Texas," *The Quarterly of the Texas State Historical Association*, Vol. XI (1907), pp. 56–66.

Williams, T. Harry: "An Analysis of Some Reconstruction Attitudes," *Journal of Southern History*, Vol. XII (1946), pp. 469–86.

Woody, Robert H.: "Franklin J. Moses, Jr., Scalawag Governor of South Carolina, 1872–1874," *The North Carolina Historical Review*, Vol. X (1933), pp. 111–32.

General Works and Special Studies—Pamphlets

Battle, William H.: *The Habeas Corpus Proceedings.* Raleigh, N.C.: Nichols and Gorman, 1870.

Beck, James B.: *Reorganization of Virginia, Mississippi and Texas.* Washington: Democratic Executive Committee, 1868.

Bromberg, Frederick G.: *The Reconstruction Period in Alabama.* Mobile, Ala. (?): Bienville Monument Fund, 1916.

Chaille, S. E.: *Intimidation and the Number of White and Colored Voters in Louisiana in 1876 as Shown by Statistical Data Derived from Republican Official Reports.* New Orleans, La.: Picayune, 1877.

Debate on the Hamburg Massacre, in the United States House of Representatives, July 15th and 18th, 1876. N.p., n.d.

Furlong, Charles E.: *Origin of the Outrages at Vicksburg.* Vicksburg, Miss.: Herald, 1874.

Proceedings of the Tax-Payer's Convention of South Carolina, 1871. Charleston, S.C.: Edward Perry, 1874.

Proceedings of the Tax-Payer's Convention of South Carolina, 1874. Charleston, S.C.: News and Courier, 1874.

Rogers, Andrew J.: *A White Man's Government.* Washington: Constitutional Union, 1866.

The Southern Question: The Bourbon Conspiracy to Rule or Destroy the Nation. N.p., n.d.

Tillman, Benjamin R.: *The Struggles of 1876: How South Carolina was Delivered from Carpetbag and Negro Rule.* N.p., n.d.

Warmoth, Henry C.: *Letter of H. C. Warmoth, Claimant of a Seat in the House of Representatives as a Delegate from the Territory of Louisiana.* Washington: McGill and Witherow, 1866.

Wilmer, J. P. B.: *A Defense of Louisiana.* New Orleans, La.: Gresham, n.d.

Index

for governor, 17; describes conditions in Tennessee, 18; mobilizes troops, 35; mentioned, 6, 19, 25 n., 31 n., 43 n., 112 n., 150

Brownsville, Tenn.: 46

Buckalew, Charles R.: opposes repeal of Militia Act, 7 n.

Butler, Benjamin F.: 84

Butler, M. C.: and Hamburg riot, 140; mentioned, 43, 133 n.

Caldwell, Charles: murder of, 125–26; mentioned, 93, 97

Caldwell, Mrs. Charles: 126 n.

Camp Holden, North Carolina: 47

Campaign of 1875 (Mississippi): 87–99, 118, 141

Campaign of 1876 (South Carolina): 133 n., 137 n., 139 n.

Cannon: used to intimidate militia, 118–19

Cardoza, T. W.: 87, 89

Carpetbaggers: in Arkansas, 52

Carter, George W.: expelled as Speaker of House, 69; loses to Warmoth, 71; mentioned, 68, 70

Carter-Warmoth feud: 14, 68–71

Casey, J. F.: 68, 73 n.

Caswell County, North Carolina: 122

Catterson, R. F.: supports Brooks, 53; mentioned, 41, 44

Chamberlain, Daniel H.: and Negro militia in South Carolina, 15; attempt to disband White Leagues, 143; mentioned, 134 n., 136

Chambers, S. L.: 108

Charleston, S.C.: 121

Chase, G. K.: report by, 141; mentioned, 97

Chesnut, James: testimony of, 46 n., 48 n.

Civil war in Arkansas: 50, 55–65

Claiborne, Miss.: White League in, 94

Clarke, Charles W.: 92 n.

Clarke, William G.: 29

Clayton, John M.: murder of, 34

Clayton, Powell: use of militia by, 13, 35; attempts to secure militia arms, 28, 119–20; speech by, 32; declares martial law, 39, 50; elected governor, 50; inauguration of, 50; enters

Nordhoff, Charles: 3

Norris Township, South Carolina: 134

North Carolina: militia violence in, 14–15; Kirk-Holden War in, 15, 41, 123, 148; militia bill of 1868, 20 n.; militia exemption tax in, 21; militia laws in, 21; Kirk forces of, 35–36, 47; Ku Klux Klan in, 14, 123; mentioned, 8, 15, 35 n., 36, 115

North Carolina State Militia: 117–18

Ogden, Frederick Nash: commander of Louisiana State Militia, 77, 78; in militia battle of September 14, 1874, 78; mentioned, 78 n., 133 n.

Olivier, Arthur: arrest of, 74

Opelousas, La.: riot in, 67; White League in, 74

Opelousas Courier (Louisiana): 135

Orange County Ku Klux Klan (North Carolina): 123

Packard, Stephen B.: claims governorship in 1876, 79–80; collapse of government of, 80; United States consul, 80; mentioned, 68

Packard-Nicholls struggle: in Louisiana, 14, 79–80

Packer, A. G.: 84, 92

Palarm Creek ambush (Arkansas): 63

Panola Star (Mississippi): 114

Parker, Kate: 135

"Peace Agreement" (Mississippi): 14, 82, 97–98

Pemberton Monument (Vicksburg, Miss.): militia battle at, 85

Penn, D. B.: runs for lieutenant governor, 72; calls up militia, 77; temporary governor, 78; mentioned, 75

People's Club: *see* White League

Physicians: in militia, 27

Pierrepont, Edwards: 92 n., 97, 141 n.

Pike County, Mississippi: 93

Pinchback, P. B. S.: supports Warmoth, 68; deserts Warmoth, 72; calls out militia, 73; installed as governor, 73

Pine Bluff, Ark.: H. King White in, 62; mentioned, 57

Porter, Horace: 44

Presidential election of 1868: 36

"Protection papers": 45

Pulaski County, Arkansas: martial law in, 55

Pulaski County Court (Arkansas): declares Brooks governor, 53

Rainey, James: 127

Rape: militiamen involved in cases of, 44

Reconstruction Act: passage of, 6

Reconstruction acts: state governments organized under, 6–7; effect of in Louisiana, 68; mentioned, 9

Red Shirts: *see* White League

Reed, Harrison: and militia in Florida, 12; attempt to secure militia arms, 28, 120; mentioned, 146

Report of the Committee on Lawlessness (Texas): 18

Republican party: in Alabama, 12; Liberal Republican revolt in, 51; in Arkansas, 51–65; in Louisiana state convention of 1871, 68

Revels, Hiram: in United States Senate, 82, 83

Rice, B. F.: advocates repeal of Militia Act, 8

Rickman, W. O.: 43

Rifle clubs: titles of, 143; mentioned, 121, 131, 133, 136, 137–38, 144; *see also* White League

"Ring" (Hamburg, S. C.): 140

Rogersville, Tenn.: 112

Rose, T. E.: quarrel with H. King White, 60–61; mentioned, 55

Rose, U.: 45 n.

Rousseau, Lovell: 67 n.

Sabre clubs: 133

"Safeguards": 45

St. Louis, Mo.: 55

Savannah, Ga.: 121

Schurz, Carl: Southern tour of, 5

Scott, Robert K.: militia of, 15, 42; speech by, 17; secures arms for militia, 29; arms militia in election of 1870, 36; administration of, 124; use of militia money by, 149–50; mentioned, 37 and n., 105 n., 110 n., 150

ter, 56, 57; quarrel with Rose, 60–61; and New Gascony encounter, 63

White League: in Alabama, 12; in Louisiana, 14, 66, 73–75, 77–78, 144; in New Orleans, La., 66, 77–78; in Claiborne, Miss., 94; movement, 129–44; purpose of, 130–33, 135; in South Carolina, 143

White Line: *see* White League

White Man's Party: *see* White League

Williams, George H.: 54, 64

Williams, I. C.: 22 n., 23 n.

Williams, Jim: murder of, 126–27

Williams, John: 27

Williams, John J.: 53 n.

Wilshire, W. W.: 58 n.

Winsmith, J.: 37 n.

Woodruff, William E.: 56

Yanceyville, N.C.: 47

Yazoo City, Miss.: martial law in, 89; pre-election violence in, 89–90; White League in, 137; mentioned, 37, 141

Yazoo Banner (Yazoo City, Miss.): 89

Yazoo City Herald (Mississippi): 91

Yocum, B. G.: 22 n.

Yorkville, S.C.: 46

CPSIA information can be obtained at www.ICGtesting.com
Printed in the USA
LVOW081129090512

280721LV00003B/1/P